nneth B. Mulholland

Adventures in Training the Ministry

A Honduran case study in theological education by extension

With a foreword by F. Ross Kinsler

ADVENTURES IN TRAINING THE MINISTRY

STUDIES IN THE WORLD CHURCH AND MISSIONS
Harvey M. Conn, *Editor*
Associate Professor of Missions and Apologetics
Westminster Theological Seminary

Planting and Development of Missionary Churches — John L. Nevius
Bringing God's News to Neighbors — Carl Kromminga
Theological Perspectives on Church Growth — ed. Harvie M. Conn
The Kalimantan Kenyah — William Conley

ADVENTURES IN TRAINING THE MINISTRY
A Honduran Case Study in Theological Education by Extension

by

Kenneth Mulholland

with

Foreword by F. Ross Kinsler

PRESBYTERIAN AND REFORMED PUBLISHING COMPANY
1976

Dedicated to

the Glory of the Triune God

and

my greatest teachers

my wife Ann

Dr. Alfred C. Bartholomew

the congregations of Bethel U.C.C. Charge

the students of the Theological Institute in Honduras

GLOSSARY OF ABBREVIATIONS

AADET   The Andes Association of Theological Education.

AATS   American Association of Theological Schools.

ABET   The Bolivian Association of Theological Schools.

AETTE   Brazilian Evangelical Theological Association for Extension Training.

ALET   Latin American Association of Theological Schools—Northern Region.

ALFALIT   An inter-church agency sponsoring literacy and primary education.

ALISTE   The Latin American Association of Institutes and Seminaries by Extension.

ASIT   The South American Association of Theological Institutions.

ASTE   The Association of Theological Seminaries in Brazil.

CAMEO   Committee to Assist Missionary Education Overseas, a joint committee of EFMA and IFMA.

CATA   Advisory Committee on Self-teaching Texts.

CET   Center of Theological Studies located in Quito, Ecuador.

CLATT   The Latin American Committee for Theological Texts.

EFMA   The Evangelical Foreign Mission Association.

IFMA   The Interdenominational Foreign Missions Association.

TEE   Theological Education by Extension.

TEF   The Theological Education Fund.

UNICO   The Union of Biblical Institutions of Greater Colombia.

vi

TABLE OF CONTENTS

LIST OF DIAGRAMS

FOREWORD

As I write these words from Alajuela, Costa Rica, a historic meeting is taking place between the Northern Region of the Latin American Theological Schools (ALET) and the Latin American Association of Institutes and Theological Seminaries by Extension (ALISTE). Out of this confrontation it has become clear that theological education by extension has gained a hearing in virtually all circles of Protestant Christianity, not only in Latin America, but worldwide. It is equally evident that the potentialities and problems of the movement need to be explored much more deeply.

The concept of theological education by extension is understood in different ways by different people. Is it a method, a system, a technology? Or is it a movement, a philosophy of preparation in ministry, a vision of the church and its mission? For some it appears as if extension is a set formula rather than an ongoing search for a vehicle of change and renewal.

Perhaps the greatest challenge of the extension movement is to keep open the door to new alternatives, new dimensions, and new insights in theological education rather than become satisfied with partial successes and limited advances. Those who are involved in extension work need to go beyond the excitement of new structures with rapidly growing numbers of grassroots leaders to a careful analysis of the theological, pedagogical, and ideological processes. TEE has spread around the world so rapidly that it has sometimes taken on the characteristics of a packaged panacea and at times been in danger of narrow alignment with certain ecclesiological and missiological perspectives. But now widely divergent traditions are discussing and experimenting with extension. And all are becoming increasingly aware of the current revolution affecting all fields and aspects of education, secular as well as theological.

One major problem is that, unfortunately, theological education by extension has too often been promoted by people and organizations that have little or no field experience with an extension program. Thus, unlike this volume, which contains a detailed case study of the author's experience, much of the literature lacks the realism and self-criticism that comes out of field experience.

This book is a significant contribution to our understanding of theological education by extension. It will enable those who are involved in the extension movement to think through the issues raised here. It will allow newcomers to get a comprehensive, incisive picture of the basic concepts.

Ken Mulholland is well equipped for this task. An outstanding young churchman of many talents and responsibilities, he is not widely known as a promoter of extension, but is one of its more experienced practitioners. During three years—1968 through 1970— he organized, directed, and taught in the extension program of the Evangelical and Reformed Church in Honduras. In recent years he has worked with extension programs in Costa Rica. He is critical of traditional patterns of theological education, yet writes from his current position as chairman of the Department of Christian Ministry and director of Field Education at the Latin American Biblical Seminary, probably the most important Protestant seminary in Latin America today and basically a residence institution. He is well aware of the multiple problems of theological education in the Third World and is convinced that the extension movement offers significant answers to these problems.

It is my hope that both the author and his readers will continue their search for new and improved patterns of theological education that will open the ministry to the whole body of Christ.

F. Ross Kinsler
June, 1975

ACKNOWLEDGMENTS

No book is a one-man effort. And this is certainly no exception! Acknowledgments must begin with Dr. Al Bartholomew, who first guided my S.T.M. research on the subject of theological education by extension and has been a constant source of encouragement to me throughout my ministry both in the United States and abroad.

Next on the list comes J. Kenneth Trauger, seminary roommate who later became a staunch colleague in Honduras. . . .

Then Dr. F. Ross Kinsler, who first fired my interest in TEE and guided my first faltering steps, for his immense patience and many helpful suggestions on the manuscript as well as for writing the foreword. . . .

And Harvie Conn, whose wonderful letter encouraged me finally to get serious about writing this book and whose editorial labors "made straight the rough places. . . ."

Sincere thanks are also due to John Kenyon, whose stylistic suggestions and hand-written "ho-hum" comments in the margins of certain pages not only made this book more readable, but also made me more objective about my writing ability; and to Linda Holland, whose keen mind deciphered my chicken scratching while her flying fingers typed the manuscript.

There is always an unnamed host of people whose contributions along the way have stimulated, enriched, informed: a host of missionary and national colleagues; present and former students in Costa Rica and Honduras; former parishioners in Pennsylvania and California.

I am also indebted to the United Church Board for World Ministries and the many individuals and congregations which undergird both spiritually and materially our ministry in Central America.

A major acknowledgment goes to my good-natured and long-suffering offspring—Christine, David, and Kathy—who shared their daddy with his extension students in Honduras, trudged through the snow drifts to accompany him to the library in Lancaster, and held the fort in Costa Rica so capably during the two weeks he spent in Guatemala putting the finishing touches on this book.

And finally, to my wife, Ann, whose love and understanding is the greatest encouragement anyone could ask for in this world and with whom I share the hope of spending eternity together in the presence of Him "who loved us and washed us from our sins by his blood, and made us a kingdom, priests to his God and Father, to him be glory and dominion for ever and ever. Amen."

INTRODUCTION

In Latin America theological education by extension has emerged not only as a viable supplement to traditional residence training, but also as a valid and valuable form of ministerial training in its own right. This conviction grows not only out of extensive reading, but through personal conversation and correspondence with the leaders of the movement, as well as personal experience in the operation of such a system in the Republic of Honduras.

The first section of this book begins with a survey of the factors converging upon theological education in Latin America today. The traditional pattern is defined, placed in its historical setting, and summoned before the tribunal of theological, numerical, and qualitative evaluation. Then it is seen in the context of the anthropological, economic, and educational aspects of the Latin American reality. Finally, alternative systems of theological education are described and evaluated, with special reference to the basic principles of theological education by extension.

The second section traces the development of theological education by extension from its beginnings in Guatemala a decade ago through its rapid growth in Latin America to a worldwide phenomenon. Reference is also made to its possible application to the North American scene.

The third section, highly subjective, is a first-person account of the attempt to develop a program of theological education by extension in the Evangelical and Reformed Synod of Honduras.

The final section describes the relationship between various important aspects of theological education as they bear upon extension: church growth, pre-theological education, accreditation, the role of the teacher, and the relationship between residence and extension study.

This book, which grew out of an S.T.M. thesis presented to the faculty of the Lancaster Theological Seminary in 1971, is offered in the sincere desire that it will stimulate theological educators throughout the world to do the hard thinking and take the decisive action necessary to better equip the whole people of God for the ministries to which God has called them.

Part I

Factors Converging on Theological Education
in Latin America Today

Chapter I

THE WAY WE'VE ALWAYS DONE IT

Theological education is all of the systematic biblical and doctrinal teaching, both theoretical and practical, that has as its purpose the preparation of the believer, especially the leader, for the role of a special ministry in the Church.

What are the factors which combine to mold theological education among Protestants in contemporary Latin America? The purpose of this first section is to evaluate critically the predominant traditional pattern in the light of the Latin American reality and explore viable alternatives with special focus upon theological education by extension.

Until the decade of the 1960's theological education in Latin America generally sought to duplicate the accepted pattern prevailing in North America or Europe—with slight variations depending upon the origin of the missionary group.[1]

Generally speaking, that pattern consisted of extracting young, unproven, single, usually male volunteers from their home environment to train them in a centrally located institution, where they resided for about three years. There they were taught the classic theological subjects, mostly by rote, by predominantly missionary professors and a sprinkling of part-time nationals. Academic training was supplemented by practical work assignments in local churches with various degrees of supervision. After three years these young people were declared pastoral material if they had successfully passed

---

1. This is quite apparent in Yorke Allen, Jr., *A Seminary Survey* (New York: Harper & Brothers Publishers, 1960), and Wildred Scopes, ed., *The Christian Ministry in Latin America and the Caribbean* (New York: Commission of World Mission and Evangelism, World Council of Churches, 1962).

the required exams, had expounded no heresy, and had not strayed beyond the bounds of morally acceptable behavior as defined by the sponsoring institution and/or denomination.[2]

Because this pattern was accepted as normative, the recommendations that came forth from various ecclesiastical bodies called for a refining and upgrading of the educational process rather than for any basic re-evaluation of this pattern of traditional theological education, despite the fact that this pattern did not originate in the United States until about 1800 and was not considered normative on a wide scale until the latter part of the nineteenth century. Until then patterns of theological education were diverse.

DEVELOPMENT: CLUES FROM THE PERSPECTIVE OF HISTORY

An examination of this diversity reveals three patterns of ministerial training which, although finally superseded by the theological seminary, were viable and appropriate patterns of theological education at one time in the history of the development of the North American Protestant Church. A study of these patterns in their historical context may furnish us with valuable clues for viable ministerial training in twentieth-century Latin America. They can help us formulate an answer to the question: What are the culturally relevant forms of theological education appropriate to the present stage of development of the Latin American Protestant Movement?

---

2. At the annual meeting of the Latin American Association of Theological Schools—Northern Region in Managua, Nicaragua, in January, 1969, James H. Emery defined a traditional seminary as ". . . the system of ministerial preparation that was developed in the United States at the beginning of the last century to provide training within the denomination. The system involves resident students who are single and young (with some special arrangements for married people). The classes are arranged according to a schedule that occupies the morning hours especially, when professors who are specialists in their fields have the lectures. There is limited discussion, the students have assigned reading and papers to prepare and can only spend a very limited time working to support themselves. A high level of academic preparation is required for entering in order to have a broad general background, but no experience is required." "The Traditional and the Extension Seminary: Conflict or Cooperation—Friends or Enemies?" *Theological Education by Extension* (South Pasadena, Calif.: William Carey Library, 1969), p. 219.

Those patterns which we shall proceed to examine briefly are apprenticeship among the Congregationalists, in-service training among the Methodists, and the "tent making" ministry among the Baptists, particularly in the South.

Apprenticeship

In keeping with their Puritan heritage, the Congregational and Presbyterian churches of English and Scottish origin continued to place a strong emphasis upon an educated clergy. Therefore, before entering upon apprenticeship, a broad general education was necessary for a clergymen who —

> . . . not infrequently was called upon to serve as schoolmaster to the parish children, and occasionally might be prevailed upon to utilize his spare time for the instruction of adults as well. . . . Nor was it unusual for a clergyman to be licensed to practice medicine, and whether licensed or not he was expected to keep a book of "physic" at hand and his wife a garden of medicinal herbs so that help could be given in emergencies. In similar fashion, he needed at least an elementary knowledge of law, for as the educated person in the community he was called upon to give legal advice, draft legal documents, and frequently to adjudicate legal disputes. In the midst of all this, if his income was to be at all adequate, he needed a moderate knowledge of farming and, in some cases, had to be able to handle a plow and spade with reasonable skill.[3]

It was precisely this concern which led to the founding of Harvard College in 1636, upon whose gateway are written the words ". . . one of the . . . things wee longed for and looked after was to advance learning and perpetvate it to posterity dreading to leave an illiterate ministry to the chvrches when ovr present ministers shall lie in the dvst."[4]

Although the Puritan churches demanded an educated clergy throughout the colonial period, they did not make academic prowess the only requisite for ordination. Upon graduation from college,

---

3. H. Richard Niebuhr and Daniel D. Williams, eds., *The Ministry in Historical Perspective* (New York: Harper & Row, Publishers, 1956), pp. 183-84.

4. Robert L. Kelley, *Theological Education in America* (New York: Charles H. Doran Company, 1924), pp. 23-24.

where he received a liberal education supplemented with biblical and theological studies, the candidate had to present himself before the duly appointed church officials in order to be licensed to preach. Once licensed, he sought a congregation which would call him as their pastor. Once called to a particular congregation he was ordained and took up his duties among the congregation which had called him, probably to remain there for life.

The licensing examination was not a routine affair. In addition to presenting his college degree, the candidate was expected to present several written sermons to the examining body and to be able to defend not only his sermons, but his entire theological system to the satisfaction of the group. For this reason few presented themselves for licensure immediately upon graduation from college. Most spent one to three years more in residence at the college under a tutor, at home on the farm, as a schoolteacher, or as an assistant to a pastor, all the while seeking to master the content of the Bible and a system of divinity as well as to write sermons in the fashion of theological dissertations.

As time passed the apprentice system became more and more the norm. A ". . . close examination shows that the Colonial colleges were more like elementary or junior-high-level boarding schools and that specific training for the ministry took place after the period of full time training in 'college,' in a kind of apprenticeship: graduates went to live in a minister's home. . . ."[5]

A candidate sought a respected and effective pastor with whom to live. He read his books, followed him around on pastoral calls, conversed with him, imbibed the cooking and counsel of the minister's wife (and perhaps received the hand of the daughter of the manse in marriage), and performed pastoral duties under watchful supervision until he was deemed worthy to serve his own congregation. Then he presented himself to the examining committee.

As more and more students flocked to men who had proven themselves wise mentors, the demands upon the elder pastor became such

---

5. Ralph D. Winter, "An Extension Seminary Manual," *Theological Education by Extension,* p. 386.

a burden that these men tended to be set apart for the full-time task of training the students gathered around them. Thus sprang into existence the so-called "schools of the prophets." Meanwhile, as the colleges became increasingly less influenced by theology and more and more given to preparing men for professions other than the clergy, these schools of the prophets expanded until they became denominational seminaries.[6]

In-Service Training

Another system of ministerial training was that employed by the Methodists, who licensed men of very limited formal education provided that they displayed the requisite spiritual fervor. In the United States a century ago the most common path of specifically ministerial preparation among the Methodists was not primarily a matter of formal education.

> A candidate for the Methodist ministry, in regard to the learning that comes from books, was not required nor as yet expected to spend three years in a post-graduate seminary. The ecclesiastical structure—the conference—had courses of study with prescribed texts, and the student was expected to study mainly on his own and pass comprehensive examinations.[7]

Methodist theological education was in-service training. Despite the extensive traveling required to cover their circuits, Methodist preachers were expected to study five hours each day and were provided with a list of specified theological works of high quality to be read. In many cases reports and examinations were required. Even Peter Cartright, known more for his crude eloquence than for his polished erudition, writes that William M'Kendree, his presiding elder and

---

6. Christopher Jencks and David Riesman, *The Academic Revolution* (New York: Doubleday & Company, Inc., 1968), p. 208, contend, "The first separate theological seminary was founded in 1784 by the Dutch Reformed Church adjacent to its undergraduate college in New Jersey." Ralph R. Covell and C. Peter Wagner also claim that the first separate theological seminary in America was founded by the Dutch Reformed Church, but give 1774 as the date and Flatbush, Long Island, New York, as the place. *An Extension Primer* (South Pasadena, Calif.: William Carey Library, 1971), p. 58. Still other sources claim that Andover, founded in 1808, was the first denominational seminary.
7. Winter, *op. cit.,* p. 409.

under whose guidance and instruction he had begun his ministry—

> . . . directed me to a proper course of reading and study. He selected books for me, both literary and theological; and every quarterly visit he made, he examined into my progress and corrected my errors, if I had fallen into any. He delighted to instruct me in English grammar.[8]

Methodist circuit riders served while they studied and studied while they served. Each one was in reality a little bishop over the congregations of his circuit, each of which was under the direction of a resident lay leader who was part and parcel of the community in which he lived.

Cartright himself believed that ". . . this way of training while already in the ministry, wherein men could (both) learn and practice every day . . ." was more advantageous than "all the colleges and Biblical institutes in the land."[9] Even as late as 1879, Alfred Brunson, a younger contemporary of Cartright who had come to Wisconsin in the 1830's was still not covinced that there was "anything superior to our old mode of training preachers IN the work rather than FOR the work."[10]

Tent-making Ministry

The early Baptists, particularly those in the South, had neither the apprenticeship system of the Puritans nor the in-service training program of the Methodists. Like the Mennonites and other groups deeply influenced by the left wing of the Reformation, the local congregation simply selected from among themselves the most gifted person to serve as pastor. Sometimes with and sometimes without the consultation of neighboring Baptist churches they proceeded to ordain him. The pastor continued to earn all or part of his living from his secular vocation unless the congregation grew to such proportions as to demand his services on a full-time basis. Because this pattern of part-time ministry was employed by the Apostle Paul, who supple-

---

8. Niebuhr and Williams, *op. cit.,* p. 240.
9. *Ibid.*
10. *Ibid.,* p. 313. Cited in footnote.

mented the gifts he received from the churches by making tents, it is sometimes termed a tent-making ministry.

Because the Baptists did not have the connectional system employed by the Methodists, local pastors depended upon self-directed study—usually of the Bible and a compend of theology—to receive a theological education. However, in many larger towns and cities when a man aspired to be a full-time pastor rather than having a tent-making ministry, a more experienced pastor apprenticed him for a period of time before he became a candidate for a vacant congregation.

Dillenberger and Welch relate how each of these patterns of theological education fared during the period of the expansion of Protestantism in the United States.

> . . . the influence of the churches was weak on the frontier. Frontier towns were small and isolated. It was impossible to provide either clergy or churches for all of the communities. Congregationalists and Presbyterians, who insisted upon an educated clergy, were particularly hard pressed. . . . Methodists were generally more successful, since they organized small groups in "classes" with a lay leader in charge, just as Wesley had done. "Classes" and Methodist communities were then visited by a Methodist minister who traveled an extensive circuit of such groups. But the Baptists were generally in the best position. In addition to having fought for political and religious freedom, they did not have the burden of a highly educated ministry. A Baptist preacher was one who felt the call. Once the decision had been made, preaching could begin. Moreover, such preachers were of the same social class of the people to whom they preached.[11]

This thumbnail survey of theological education reveals that apprenticeship, in-service training, and tent-making ministries were widely used patterns in the United States at one time; indeed, that the predominant pattern at one time was training in ministry rather than training for ministry. Furthermore, it was precisely those denominations which recognized, set apart, and equipped the natural leaders of the common people for the work of ministry which were best able

---

11. John Dillenberger and Claude Welch, *Protestant Christianity Interpreted through Its Development* (New York: Charles Scribner's Sons, 1954), p. 148.

to respond to the turbulence, the mobility, and the poverty of the American frontier. In time it was the Methodists and Southern Baptists, with their flexible and culturally relevant patterns of ministerial selection and training, rather than the Congregationalists and Presbyterians, which became the predominant religious bodies of the North American continent.

This insight provides important clues not only for Latin American theological education, but for theological education in many developing nations. The tendency of North American theological educators is to seek to impose those models of theological education which are most current in North Atlantic countries upon the developing nations rather than explore models which were viable in those same countries when they historically faced some of the same problems which the Third World nations now confront. While upgrading the academic level of the clergy may be the solution for a stagnant church in a highly educated and affluent culture where the number of clergy is roughly equal to the number of congregations, it is decidedly not the solution for a growing church in a largely illiterate and poverty-stricken culture where there are five congregations or more to every clergyman. Thus, referring to Chile, Christian LaLive d'Epinay writes, ". . . the educational institutions and methods applicable in Europe or the U.S.A. are not suitable for the needs in Chile. . . ."[12]

The issue must be faced: Is it not better that many churches have some modestly trained leadership than that a few churches have highly trained leadership and the rest have no trained leadership at all?

This issue is not unique to the church. In the burgeoning cities of the Third World, one finds an abundance of medical personnel on a professional par with those in the Northern Hemisphere nations—lacking only some of the advanced equipment and extreme specialization necessary to treat extremely rare diseases. On the other hand, in the rural areas, where one finds the majority of the population, there are almost no doctors, no lawyers, no nurses, and few teachers. For instance, in the predominantly rural nation of Guatemala, 1,025

---

12. Christian LaLive d'Epinay, "The Training of Pastors and Theological Education: The Case of Chile," *The International Review of Missions* LVI (1967), p. 191.

out of the 1,208 doctors who practice medicine exercise their profession within the capital city. That leaves only 183 for all the rest of the country! And the majority of these are concentrated in a handful of large towns![13] Yet, in the name of "maintaining standards" few if any programs are developed to train para-medical, para-legal, or para-educational personnel to meet at least partially the needs of a growing population.

Indeed, the historical perspective forces us to raise the questions loud and clear: Is it possible at this moment in history and in the context of the current situation in Latin America, that heavy dependence upon traditional theological education is not the answer to the leadership training needs of the Latin American Protestant community? Is it possible that once-useful, but now discarded patterns of ministerial training in the developed nations may provide important insights, clues, and even models upon which to construct relevant theological education for the growing churches in the developing nations, particularly Latin America?

A CRITIQUE: THREE QUESTIONS

With the clues afforded by a historical perspective, let us now bring traditional theological education before the bar of theological, numerical, and cultural criteria.

Is It Theologically Defensible?

In the early years of the twentieth century, a young Anglican missionary to China raised an uncomfortable question about theological education. To the commonly debated question of his day, "Is the pattern of a full-time academically trained professional clergy possible on a large scale in the younger churches?," he added the brutal interrogative, "Is it even desirable?" Like his contemporaries P. T. Forsyth in the field of systematic theology and James Denney in the field of biblical studies, Roland Allen was a man born ahead of his time. It is only in the past decade that his writings, long out of print, have been republished and widely circulated—strangely enough by

13. "Desproporción Medica," *Prensa Libre,* Guatemala, February 11, 1972, p. 14.

those who do not necessarily share his churchly point of view.

Of all his writings perhaps the most significant which bears upon the issue under discussion is the book, *The Case for Voluntary Clergy*.[14] Allen in no way desired the abolition of the full-time professional, or "stipendary" clergy as he termed them, but urgently longed for the recognition of voluntary clergy as full ministers of the Gospel. Thus he called for "the ordination . . . of men who maintain themselves by their own trade and profession."[15] In modern terminology he desired an ordained "tent-making" ministry. Allen wasted no time in laying his cards on the able:

> My contention in this book is that the tradition which we hold, forbidding the ordination of men engaged in earning their own livelihood by what we call secular occupations, makes void the word of Christ and is opposed to His mind when He instituted the sacraments for His people. It is also opposed to the conception of the Church which the apostles received from Him and to the practice by which St. Paul, of whose work God has given us the fullest account, established the churches. The stipendary system grew up in settled churches and is suitable for settled churches at some periods; for expansion, for the establishment of new churches it is the greatest possible hindrance. It binds the church in chains and has compelled us to adopt practices which contradict the very idea of the Church.[16]

Allen goes on to condemn the stipendary system—the practice of having *only* a paid, full-time professional clergy—as being without "biblical authority and . . . not the doctrine of the gospel . . . ," but ". . . a burden. . . ."[17]

---

14. *The Case for Voluntary Clergy*, containing over 300 pages and now very rare, was published in 1930. It incorporated in revised form the substance of two earlier books: *Voluntary Clergy* and *Voluntary Clergy Overseas*. The selection upon which I base this section of my thesis is found in the book edited by David M. Paton, *The Ministry of the Spirit: Selected Writings of Roland Allen* (Grand Rapids: William B. Eerdmans, 1960), and consists of selected quotations from chapters 1-3, 5-7, 10, 11, 13, 15, 18, and 22 of the original work.

15. David M. Paton, ed., *The Ministry of the Spirit: Selected Writings of Roland Allen*, p. 137.

16. *Ibid.*

17. *Ibid.*

After reaffirming his position that the ordination of voluntary clergy is "a truth of Christ which demands obedience . . . ," he turns to an examination of such biblical passages as I Timothy 3:2-7 and Titus 1:6-9, where he defines "bishops" as synonymous with "elders" and to whom he attributes the pastoral office. Citing Acts 14:23, he observes that when St. Paul and his followers ordained elders in every city, the men whom they ordained were not lower clergy being ordained to higher office, but rather men who previously had not been ordained to any sacred ministry whatsoever.

Upon analysis of the above-mentioned biblical passages on the requirements of spiritual leaders, Allen is struck by the great emphasis placed upon moral qualities for leadership:

> Of the fifteen items in the first passage, five are personal virtues, six are social virtues, one is moral intellectual, one is experience, and two are concerned with reputation. Five are personal virtues: temperate, soberminded, orderly, gentle, not a lover of money. Six are social virtues: ruling the children well, given to hospitality; secondly, abroad as well as at home; no brawler, no striker, not contentious. Two refer to reputation: in the eyes of non-Christians. One is a moral intellectual power: apt to teach. One is experience: not a novice.[18]

Turning to the second passage, Allen finds that

> . . . there are fifteen items of which eight are personal virtues; not self-willed, not soon angry, not greedy of filthy lucre, lover of good, sober minded, just, holy, temperate. Four are social virtues: constant to one wife, given to hospitality, no brawler, no striker. One refers to home conditions; having faithful children who are not accused of riot or unruly. One refers to reputation: blameless. One is a moral intellectual qualification: holding to the faithful word; to which is attached a power to exhort in the sound doctrine and to convict gainsayers.[19]

Allen concludes that in both passages the same emphasis is placed upon the primacy of moral qualities followed by the social virtues, both in the home and in the community at large.

Then in one of the most gripping passages in his work, for one

---

18. *Ibid.*, p. 139.
19. *Ibid.*, pp. 139-40.

who has served the Church overseas, he writes: "Anyone who has been in the mission field will instantly recognize the portrait. The man lives before our eyes. . . ."[20] Allen goes on to paint a word picture of this spiritual leader whom he feels the church should recognize by conferring upon him ordination.

> He is a man of mature age, the head of a family. He has been married long enough to have children who are old enough to believe, and to be capable of riotous and unruly conduct. His wife and children and household are well governed and orderly. He is a man of some position in the community. Strangers and visitors, especially Christians on their journeys are naturally directed to his house and he knows how to entertain them and can do so. He is a man of certain gravity and dignity whose words carry weight. He can teach and rebuke those who would slight the exhortations of a lesser man. He is a man of moral character; he can rule without violence He has no temptation to be always dealing blows, because his moral authority is sufficient to secure obedience. He is sober-minded and just; he can settle disputes with a judgment which men respect; and he is not ready to take a bribe. He is a Christian of some standing. He has learned the teaching of the apostles and he holds it fast. He can teach what he has learned and when someone propounds a strange doctrine, or a morally doubtful course of action, he can say; "that is not in accord with what I was taught"; and men listen to him and pay heed to what he says.[21]

And Allen is right. That man does live before our eyes. During the time I spent in Honduras, five new congregations of the Evangelical and Reformed Church were organized. In each case it was primarily the kind of man Allen describes who served as the key person in the birth of the new congregation. I once translated into Spanish the quotation cited above and read it to my students in Honduras. I asked them to make a list of the men who passed before their eyes as I read. Amazingly, their lists matched perfectly! And significantly, their lists included more lay leaders of local congregations than ordained preachers, many of whom were not mentioned at all by the students.

---

20. *Ibid.*, p. 140.
21. *Ibid.*

Who were some of these men? They saw before their eyes Reyes in Las Vegas. Seventy years old, a touch of deafness, a third-grade education, a single year of Bible school, and humble dress combine to belie the fact that this man has taught himself to play four musical instruments by ear and can expound the Bible with such earnestness and simplicity spiced with homespun illustrations and experiences that his counsel is sought by young and old alike. They respect his integrity and his humble, disciplined life, which, bordering on the sacrificial, speaks to them of profound commitment and genuine discipleship. In a rough, bustling mining community, he has built up from nothing a congregation of 60, many of whom are young, and several of whom are tithers. They have built and paid for their own brightly painted church building and are now paying for a modest frame parsonage which is a marked improvement over the one room that formerly served as manse.

They saw before their eyes Esteban—forty years old and the father of a large family. Esteban was a mason in a rural village before securing a job as janitor of the mission high school. Unassuming, underweight, shabbily dressed, but with piercing black eyes that radiate the alertness expressive of his innate intelligence, Esteban, who never had the opportunity to go beyond the fifth grade, was the moving force in his poverty-stricken village of San Buenaventura as he won many of his larger family to affirm publicly evangelical faith in Christ. Many come to hear him teach the Bible with direct application to their daily lives. They know that Esteban's own life squares with what he teaches. Five years ago the congregation erected a chapel, three years ago they added a thatched Sunday school addition, two years ago they were formally organized and received into Synod. Presently, the congregation has provided the leadership for the installation of a pure water system for the village.

Horacio lives in the isolated mountain village of Subirana, where he and his wife operate a small *trucha,* or grocery store. Horacio often takes lengthy trips through the mountains selling clothes from house to house. In recent years he has acquired some land and animals. In his late thirties, extremely neat and ruggedly handsome, he has gained the respect of the people not only in his own village, but throughout the mountainous area in which he lives. He displays great aptness to teach and counsel people, as well as administrative astuteness learned from the many accounts he must handle in his business.

And there are others: Andrés, a farmer and lay leader in Río Chiquito, whose son was the outstanding graduate of the Mission High School last year and who is now studying for the pastorate; Teofilo, also a farmer, who more than once has walked 20 miles to the nearest paved road in order to attend special classes at the Theological Institute and who has been instrumental in organizing a small medical clinic in his village as well as starting another preaching point nearby; Ricardo, a 60-year-old blacksmith, who although in competition with the pastor of the Central Church of Choloma, has built up a branch Sunday school from next to nothing to a congregation soon to be organized; Darias, a 30-year-old ex-communist now hard at work organizing literacy classes in connection with the branch Sunday school he superintends.

Several of the present pastors also passed before the eyes of the students that day, but significantly many were left unnamed. Then the question occurred, "Would it be better for the life of the church if some of the unordained were ordained?" It appeared that the basis of selection for ordination had not been the apostolic qualifications laid down in the Pastoral Epistles, but rather the meeting of academic qualifications by those who had been privileged to receive a full formal education.

Allen repeats,

> There, in the mission field, where Christians are scattered in little groups, a man like this stands out with a prominence which is not so easily marked at home. When we read the apostle's description of the man whom he has directed his followers to ordain, we instinctively say: We know that man.[22]

Then, having painted the portrait of the ideal candidate for ordination, Allen goes on to analyze the contradictions between that and common practice.

First, he notes that whereas the apostles demanded maturity and

22. *Ibid.*

experience on the part of the candidate, we commonly ordain the young and inexperienced.

Second, he comments that while we add the qualification that the candidate for ordination must renounce all means of livelihood other than that of the sacred ministry, there is not a trace of such a requirement among the apostolic qualifications.

Third, he observes that whereas great emphasis is placed upon a man being personally convinced of the call of God, the reality of the local church demands that equal weight be given to the congregation's call; indeed, that the call of God's people may well be a more reliable index to the moving of the Spirit than a mystical secret call. Thus, he affirms that the local church should be convinced that the candidate is truly the best man to serve. " 'If a man desire' does imply that there are men eager to be appointed, but that is quite a different matter from appealing to men to offer."[23] Allen was frankly critical of the traditional system which invited people to offer themselves before the Church had called them. He would reverse the process. The Church should single out the one whom they sense God has called, and then if that person is so convinced that the call of the Church is indeed the call of God, he is bound to respond. "Were the call of the church put first," writes Allen, "the internal vocation could respond to that."[24]

Fourth, Allen stresses, in regard to ministerial training itself, the value of the spiritual, practical training which God gives through life and experience as of more value than the formal training of his day, which he saw as one-sided.

Fifth, Allen affirms that if believers truly desire the benefits of a full life in the Church, then it ought to be possible for them to have them. This necessarily involves the ordination of the leader of the group. While Allen defines voluntary clergy as those who earn their living by the work of their hands or of their heads in the common market and who serve as clergy without stipend or fee, he makes it clear that he is not talking about "lay leaders," but of fully ordained

23. *Ibid.*, p. 143.
24. *Ibid.*, p. 144.

men set apart to preach the Word and administer the sacraments in the fullest sense of the word and whose ordination is recognized by all. Allen berates those church bodies which are willing to license such people as "workers," but which forbid them the right to administer the sacraments as well as some of the rites—especially marriage and confirmation, yet allows them to preach and preside at funerals. Such practices give a sporadic character to the total sacramental life of the Christian community, forcing it to depend upon the infrequent visitations of an ordained man. Why is it, he constantly probes, that this untrained man, who cannot be trusted to maintain the order of the church by reading a standardized liturgy, is nevertheless entrusted with the task of proclaiming the Word and teaching the Bible to a group of persons who implicitly trust his every interpretation?

Two illustrations of Allen's missionary theory come to mind out of my experience in Honduras. One is provided by the Assemblies of God. They asked a new congregation to choose a pastor from among themselves or from another congregation. This person is then licensed to perform the sacraments as well as preach the Word and is subsequently equipped to do so effectively by attending a Bible institute during four months each year over a period of six years. The congregation promises to support the pastor and his family to the best of their ability. While the ideal remains that of the full-time, paid pastor, the group normally cannot undertake his full support. Thus, he continues in his secular work full or part-time until they can provide fully for his needs. The Pentecostals see voluntary clergy and/or a tent-making ministry as a necessary, though ideally not permanent, step in the direction of the full-time pastorate.

Another example is that of the Conservative Baptists in Olanchito, Yoro, a field of work abandoned by the Evangelical and Reformed Church several years ago as an area in which it was impossible to make any progress. This evaluation appeared to be just as true for the Baptists. After 15 years of work they had only two organized congregations with 35 members. Then, in the late 1960's a new missionary, George Patterson, profoundly shaped by Allen's thinking, began to baptize believers immediately upon profession of faith, organize them into small groups, and have them select their leader on the basis of the biblical passages in the Pastoral Epistles. Those selected were duly ordained and were taught to conduct weekly worship including weekly administration of the Lord's Supper using a set liturgy with extensive Scripture passages. Most of the new pastors were capable of delivering a sermon only once a month. Simple aids were employed for the clergy, whose educational level for the most part reaches only second or third grade. Theological education takes place through small self-teaching manuals and periodic visits by the missionary to several regional centers. Here a tent-making ministry is viewed not as a theory, but as a practical necessity for years to come. Between 1967 and 1971, 22 new congregations were planted, and membership grew from 35 to 600 in the valley. It continues to grow at the rate of 25% annually. Post-baptismal dropout is extremely low.

The Evangelical and Reformed Church of Honduras, however, has steadfastly refused to ordain such voluntary clergy. Lay leaders, yes! Collaborating servants, yes! But tent-making minister, no! A man is either a volunteer worker entirely dependent on the work of his hand or head, or he is a fully supported pastor. There is no middle ground. The present discipline before the Synod for study specifically prohibits pastors from engaging in secular work. A former version even declared work outside the home as off-limits to the wives of pastors. Apparently, the feeling exists that such work is degrading to the high calling of the pastorate.

Allen's thesis is that the crying need of an expanding church around the world is the ordination of voluntary clergy as pastors in order to supplement the work of the stipendary clergy, for whether or not one receives a stipend is irrelevant by biblical-theological standards to his status and function as a clergyman.

Is It Numerically Adequate?

During the past decade those who favored the gradual upgrading and expansion of the traditional residence approach to theological education in Latin America have been challenged. The challenge is made not only on biblical-theological grounds, but on practical grounds as well—the pressing concern of the Latin American churches to train leadership for a growing church. J. Herbert Kane writes:

> Two generations ago John R. Mott stated that the greatest weakness of the missionary movement was our failure to produce well trained leaders for the national churches. Half a century has come and gone and the problem is still with us. . . . A Report of the Theological Education Fund 1964–65 states: "Grim statistics show the supply of ministers to be wholly inadequate for the number of vacant posts."[25]

Baldly stated, the problem is that the church in Latin America is growing so fast that the present institutions are simply not capable of training even the present leaders of the Protestant movement, much less the wave of future leaders.

Thomas J. Liggett summarized the findings of Read, Monterroso, and Johnson in regard to the statistical growth of Latin American Protestantism.

> In the early twentieth century the evangelical movement began to gather strength, and by 1916 the Protestant community had reached an estimated total constituency of 122,000. In 1937 the evangelical community had 1,250,000 and by 1961 it numbered an estimated 10 million. In a recent study of church growth in Latin America, careful statistics in 17 countries showed the total number of communicants to be 4,915,477. The same study estimated that the total evangelical community would be at least 14 million by 1970.[26]

The paramount importance of leadership training was underscored in a study made by World Vision, sponsored during a pastor's conference in Colombia, South America. Of the 400 men present from Colombia, Panama, Venezuela, and Ecuador, findings indicated that 31% had no schooling whatsoever, 33% had some primary schooling, 32% had finished primary school (6 grades), 26% had some second-

25. J. Herbert Kane, "Why We Are Here," *The CAMEO Workshop*. This publication is incorporated in an anthology edited by Ralph D. Winter, *Theological Education by Extension,* p. 265.

26. Thomas J. Liggett, *Where Tomorrow Struggles to Be Born: The Americas in Transition* (New York: Friendship Press, 1970), pp. 50-60. Cf. W. R. Reed, Victor M. Monterroso and Harmon A. Johnson, *Latin American Church Growth* (Grand Rapids: William B. Eerdmans, 1969).

ary school, and only 6% had completed high school. Some of this latter group also had studied at the university, and a tiny minority of these had completed their university training.[27] See Diagram A.

Commenting on these statistics, Ralph D. Winter observes:

> As low as the educational level of these local pastors is, there are another 3,000 local pastors in these four countries who unofficially fulfill the role of pastor, but did not attend. Thus the general level of education of the *average* acting pastor is no doubt a good deal lower.[28]

In the light of recent estimates that there are about 75,000 Protestant congregations in existence in Latin America with an additional 5,000 new congregations being formed each year (most of which have at least two or three preaching points), Winter continues:

> . . . there is a minimum of 150,000 with pastoral gifts, probably 90% of which seriously lack further training. But if only 100,000 of them need ministerial training this is a massive, urgent challenge. To meet this challenge there are sixty seminaries with a total enrollment of one thousand plus 300 Bible Institutes with a total enrollment of 12,000. Even assuming these students were all to become pastors, or better still were mainly men in the group of 100,000 who are already on the job, we would still be backlogged for fifteen years in meeting the need by conventional methods.[29]

Winter's analysis mentions the fact that in reality most Bible institutes are largely devoted to training Christian youth who are not necessarily pastoral material. But he fails to mention that each year approximately 5,000 new congregations are brought into existence. This means that the leadership gap instead of narrowing is actually widening. All this serves to underscore the hard reality that regardless of how one evaluates the quality of theological education in Latin America today, there is simply not enough being done even quantitatively and that the traditional system has proven itself inadequate to meet the need and is unable to expand sufficiently to offer any hope

---

27. Ralph D. Winter, "New Winds Blowing," *Church Growth Bulletin* III (July, 1967), p. 241. The diagram comes from the same article.

28. *Ibid.*

29. *Ibid.*, p. 242.

Diagram A: The Secular Education of 400 Pastors

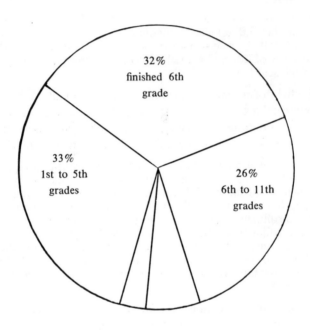

32%
finished 6th
grade

33%
1st to 5th
grades

26%
6th to 11th
grades

3%—no schooling   6%—12 grades or more

Based on a study of 400 pastors in attendance at a pastors' conference in Colombia, South America, in April, 1967. Taken from Ralph D. Winter, "New Winds Blowing," *Church Growth Bulletin* III (July, 1967), p. 241.

of doing so in the near future, particularly given the present worldwide economic crisis.

Is It Culturally Adaptable?

As it became increasingly obvious that the existing structures of theological education are inadequate to train either the actual or potential leadership for the rapidly expanding Protestant movement, some voices continued to call for a crash program to expand the existing system; but other voices began to be raised challenging the traditional pattern of theological education. They claimed that it was not more of the same system of theological education that was needed, but a different approach altogether—theological education adapted to Latin American reality. What gave added weight to the chorus of dissenters was the assent to their cause on the part of James F. Hopewell, then director of the Theological Education Fund, a man regarded as one of the most knowledgeable in the world in regard to theological education. He wrote:

> If we faced a *tabula rasa* situation in which nothing was known about the form or function of seminaries as they now exist, we probably would not create in that void a training structure that would resemble the present theological school.[30]

> Now I would like to contend, at least for the purpose of argument, that most of these factors that comprise our understanding of typical theological education have been unconsciously designed to avoid, and thereby to hinder, the basic Christian intention of mission. And I do not mean to beat the anti-intellectual drum against higher learning. What rather concerns an increasing number of critics is that the very tool of higher learning has been misappropriated to perform a third-rate job for a second-rate church structure. In a time when our understanding of the ministry more and more implies its dynamic, missionary function, we continue to rely upon a system of preparation which at its roots is essentially static and isolationist.[31]

Later, when discussing the need to train a tent-making ministry in Latin America, Hopewell despaired of traditional methods of theological education as a live option for educating a part-time clergy:

---

30. James F. Hopewell, "Mission and Seminary Structure," *The International Review of Missions* LVI (1967), p. 158.

31. James F. Hopewell, "Preparing the Candidate for Mission," *Theological Education by Extension*, p. 38. The quotation is from the text of an address made at a consultation on theological education early in 1965. The same address appears in a condensed and revised form as the lead article of the April, 1967, issue of the *International Review of Missions*, but without the passage cited.

It is increasingly apparent that any large number of tent-making ministers cannot be trained by traditional methods of theological education. Private study and apprenticeship schemes on the one hand tend to be haphazard and atomized affairs. To take, on the other hand, any quantity of mature men through the normal three to five-year residence course in a theological school and to support their families would be a luxury that most churches in the world could not afford. A traditional residence course has other disadvantages. . . .[32]

Hopewell's misgivings are echoed by many who see the traditional system as basically a foreign transplant ill adapted to Latin America except for possibly the urban professional classes. Although criticisms are numerous, they are often partial and fragmentary. These criticisms can be categorized around the following foci: student selection, academic diversity, cultural dislocation, clerical mentality, graduate placement, student dependency, drop-out percentage, and economic costliness.

Student Selection. The refrain that the traditional residence program does not train the right students is oft-repeated. Hopewell laments that the "more usual person whom the church presents to the seminary for education seems now to be the young and probably immature man who has had only minimal experience in any life other than schooling and church work.[33] James Emery charges that by its very nature of training *for service* rather than *in service* the traditional seminary ". . . limits the number of candidates to a relatively small group for reasons which do not have to do with a call or with effectiveness in the pastorate: age, education, marriage and economics" rather than "leadership ability, perseverance and spiritual gifts. . . ."[34] Writing from the standpoint of the mechanics of administration, Samuel F. Rowen adds:

The administration of a central school is very limited in its ability to select the right students who are leaders or potential leaders in

32. James F. Hopewell, "Training a Tent-Making Ministry in Latin America," *International Review of Missions* LV (1966), p. 333.
33. James F. Hopewell, "Preparing the Candidate for Mission," *Theological Education by Extension,* p. 45.
34. Emery, *op. cit.,* p. 222.

the church. . . . Therefore, the general opinion is that since there is such a great need, anyone who desires to train for the Lord's work should be sent to the school. The school will then take the recommendation of the pastor and the church concerning the character of the prospective student. The school is basically dependent upon the references it receives as to the quality of the prospective student's life and potential as a leader. On the other hand, once a student arrives at school and begins to demonstrate his ability or lack of it, it is sometimes difficult to recognize him on the basis of his recommendations. People are often unwilling to give an objective evaluation for fear of saying something against an individual who claims that he has been called by God.[35]

Rowen concludes that the central residence school by its very nature is forced into the position of selecting its students on an inadequate basis.

Academic Diversity. Traditional theological education seems incapable of the simultaneous handling of the levels of academic training necessary in Latin America now. Rowen sums up the dilemma:

Although the problem of challenging the excellent student as well as meeting the needs of the slower student is a well nigh universal problem, that problem is intensified in developing countries where there is a great disparity in the amount of training of students—sometimes from the 6th grade to university students.[36]

In this situation the tendency to aim at a middle level often spells mediocrity of instruction—too advanced for the slower students and too boring for the better students. I discovered that my own temptation was to channel my efforts into teaching the better students while allowing the slower students to fall by the wayside. "And to have different levels of instruction means additional class hours, additional teachers, additional facilities which are often overtaxing."[37] Some denominations have created separate institutions for different levels of study, but the cost is so high that these institutions could not continue to exist without heavy foreign subsidy.

---

35. Samuel F. Rowen, *The Resident Extension Seminary: A Seminary Program for the Dominican Republic* (Miami: West Indies Mission, 1967), p. 12.
36. *Ibid.,* p. 8.
37. *Ibid.,* p. 9.

Cultural Dislocation. In the United States the gap between the urban and rural mentality is markedly decreasing, but that gap remains immense in Latin America. To urbanize someone is often to make him incapable of readjusting to rural village life. Often the difference between the rural areas themselves is sufficiently marked to make it necessary to think of them in terms of subcultures. Sometimes there are even language difficulties. Rowen observes:

> The campus . . . must be located geographically. If the campus is in the rural section, then those from the urban centers find it socially degrading to receive their training in a rural setting. Likewise, if the campus is located in the urban center those from the rural districts are confronted with a radically different way of life.[38]

While it is often very difficult at first for rural students to adjust to urban life, after a few years it is even more difficult for them to readjust to the primitive conditions of rural life. Once having tasted the affluence and financial opportunities of the city, it is a real temptation for them not to return to the community from which they originally came.

When a group places all its eggs in the basket of traditional theological education the problem can be acute. A leading Latin American educator remarked that 15-year-olds brought up in the hustle and bustle of the port city of Puerto Cortes, Honduras, appeared to him to be more mature than 20-year-olds in the rural southwestern section of the country. William J. Nottingham tells of a seminary located in Argentina for the simultaneous training of both Argentinean and Brazilian candidates which uses German as a medium of instruction rather than choose between Spanish and Portuguese. And several Misquito Indians, sent by the Moravians to study in the Honduran capital of Tegucigalpa, have had traumatic—if not near fatal—experiences trying to judge distances of oncoming automobiles, having never before seen automobiles in their part of the country.

Commenting on the importance of geographical location, Hopewell laments:

---

38. *Ibid.*

An important new school of my own community, (Episcopal) Seminary of the Caribbean, seems to have been almost deliberately located near nothing at all; far away from the University of Puerto Rico, and in outer suburbia, and a sanitary distance away from the Evangelical Seminary.[39]

On the credit side, he notes that some schools ". . . have sought out the inner city, or the university, or, in Mexico City, each other on adjacent campuses." But on the debit side he observes that ". . . even in these instances there is depressingly little evidence of fruitful commerce between the seminary and the neighborhood.[40]

A final illustration of cultural dislocation, or environmental uprooting as it is sometimes termed, is the case of the Disciples of Christ and Congregationalists in Mexico. They educate the pastors for their tiny rural congregations located on the west coast of Mexico in a United Seminary at an exorbitant cost. There they live in luxurious buildings, eat in an $85,000 dining hall, and urinate in marble washrooms—all set in the wealthiest district of Mexico City. Is it any wonder that "In spite of . . . a broad ecclesiastical base, an enormous investment in buildings and professors, heavy student subsidy, and visionary plans for serious ecumenical theology, member schools . . . may have difficulty in locating their graduates in local parishes?"[41]

Clerical Mentality. Emery charges that the traditional system of theological education "tends to produce a professional orientation which separates the candidate from the common problems of the laity by placing him in an artificial category of authority and knowledge."[42] Rowen is even more precise:

After an individual has attained some formal training in a given area, there is often the tendency to develop an attitude of superiority. Once having learned the blessing and advantages of training it is often difficult for the individual to revert to the

---

39. James F. Hopewell, "Preparing the Candidate for Mission," *Theological Education by Extension,* p. 44.

40. *Ibid.*

41. Anonymous, "Extension Theological Training in Mexico," *Theological Education Newsletter* (June, 1970), p. 2.

42. Emery, *op. cit.*

simplicity he once knew. Therefore, there is the tendency to elevate oneself above the people surrounding him.[43]

This problem can become very acute when it surfaces in the life of the church. In Latin America there is a strong clerical attitude and a marked division between clergy and laity, sacred and secular, and with it a tendency on the part of the laity to foster the spirit of clericalism while at the same time verbally denouncing it.

The theological student enters school as a layman and leaves as a clergyman. Often he fancies himself as a professional, for there is great prestige in being a professional in Latin America. And being a "professional," he therefore expects better standards of living and educational opportunities which can be met only by a church accustomed to professional leadership. This syndrome produces a student who sees the ministry as a doorway to middle-class affluence, seeking the pastorate of a city congregation or leaving the pastoral ministry for the world of commerce for which in many ways his seminary training has well prepared him.

Or the obverse pattern, not of professionalism but of sanctimony, may creep in as the pastoral candidate sees himself as absolutely holy and absolutely self-denying with great power and authority surrounding him in his position of privilege. Comments Estela de Horning: "We have rejected the form of hierarchy, but we have conserved its spirit."[44]

Graduate Placement. Despite the acute shortage of trained clergy in Latin America, the placement of graduates often constitutes a critical problem.

> The most common feeling on the part of the student is that once he graduates there will be a church ready for him to pastor and that this church will provide the means of his livelihood. Though there are some churches without a full time minister, in which he can serve, yet many of these churches are not able to support a pastor because the people themselves are living very close to the subsistence level.[45]

---

43. Rowan, *op. cit.*
44. Estela de Horning, "Haciendo un Pastorado Adecuado para las Iglesias en El Ecuador," translated by this writer from a mimeographed position paper.
45. Rowen, *op. cit.*, p. 11.

The central residence school contributes to this problem in several ways.

First, since the church has required that the student be uprooted from his means of livelihood in his environment, and since upon graduation he must find a livelihood of some kind, it is only natural to think that the church which has uprooted him from his old job and trained him for a new one, will provide that job.

Second, the student has become accustomed to dependency upon the church during his studies. Most probably he has received a scholarship which covers not only tuition, but travel, medicine, room, board, and perhaps even books and clothing. It is hard to break this pattern of total dependence, especially when it is combined with a professional mentality which conditions him to expect that the church simply must make provision for him.

Third, inasmuch as his set of values has been altered by his theological education, he considers it his right to satisfy some of the desires awakened in him through the luxuries he has seen both in the city and the middle-class standard of living enjoyed by the missionaries.

The dilemma in regard to placement is existentially stated in a letter written by Herbert Schaal describing his work among the German background Congregationalists in Argentina:

> Although our present seminary has a capacity for twelve students, the actual enrollment has been lower in recent years. This is mainly due to the fact that our total financial situation does not allow the placing of more and more graduates into the field without a decent salary. Most of our graduates go to Brazil to serve at least one missionary term of six years. Thereafter, we feel morally obliged to give them a post back here in Argentina, and we cannot therefore "pour" out graduates, then after a few years "create" work and support them here.[46]

In this case the problem of placement is the problem of overproduction. The supply is greater than the demand. Rowen speaks directly to this issue when he warns of the danger of training the kind of national leadership which is beyond the capacity of the national

---

46. Herbert Schaal, "September 1970 Revision of the Fact Sheet on Our Argentina Mission," Unpublished circular letter.

church to receive or support. He feels it imperative that those called to leadership training provide not only the best possible preparation, but also the opportunities to exercise the gifts of leadership.[47]

Student Dependency. Although closely related to the development of a clerical mentality and the problem of placement, the creation of dependent persons unable to exercise leadership among their own people is a distinct problem. It appears in institutions that, while dedicated to training leaders, must do so in a context that often makes the trainee exceedingly dependent not only on the institution *qua* institution, but also on the director of the institution, often a missionary.

Melvin Hodges chronicles some of the tragic results of this syndrome and suggests some causes.[48]

First, the worker may not be able to lead the national church because the members see him as merely a front for the missionary. Therefore, they constantly appeal to the missionary over the head of the worker. At other times, if they wish to avoid the authority of the missionary as well, they go around him by appealing to a strong lay leader within the congregation.

Second, he may lack initiative. He has become accustomed to subjecting himself to the will of the missionary and so may continue to wait for the missionary to direct his work, even to the point of telling him when to visit a new locality.

Third, he may experience difficulty in adjusting himself anew to the humble surrounding of the community to which he ministers, for he "has slept on a bed. Now it is too much to expect him to sleep on a mat on the bare floor."[49]

Fourth, he may continue to depend on the missionary to meet his financial needs and be unable to demonstrate a robust faith in God to supply his every need.

> The missionary would do well to reflect that such national workers are not entirely to blame for their inadequacy. . . . The worker's training from boyhood has largely been under semi-foreign in-

---

47. Rowen, *op. cit.*
48. Melvin L. Hodges, *On the Mission Field: The Indigenous Church* (Chicago: Moody Press, 1953).
49. *Ibid.,* p. 50.

fluence and under circumstances which have separated him from his native environment. . . . Furthermore, he has been trained in Western learning rather than in the wisdom of his race. . . . Granted that he looks too much to the missionary for his support. What else could be expected? Has not the missionary always provided for him, first in school, then in his outstation work, afterwards in the seminary and finally in the pastorate. The training of his whole life has been one of dependence upon the missionary.[50]

Placing the student in an institution where he is completely dependent on others is not generally the best way to prepare persons who are later expected to be genuinely capable of exercising independent leadership.

Educational Methodology. Another source of criticism directed at traditional residence programs is the emphasis upon passive learning—a dependence upon the lecture system for imparting instruction. Despite the advances of educational psychology in terms of the value of active participation in the learning process, Emery generalizes:

> Traditionally the seminary has depended heavily upon the lecture method for the dispersal of information. Under this system the professor often spends a large portion of his time repeating material that is already in the textbook. He may allow time for discussion of the material and to clarify the problems and questions of the students.[51]

Hopewell is even more biting in his criticism:

> There is a lot of pious talk about getting away from rote training, but its practice tends to reappear more subtly in probably most lecture series now delivered, the difference being primarily that the lecturer no longer pauses long enough for his students to write each of his words verbatim. . . . The lecture principle is still worshipped to a degree approaching idolatry. . . . Honest seminars and research projects are only seldom encountered. Reading assignments are frequently considered as merely hurdles over which the student must jump before he reproduces his lecture notes for the final examination.[52]

Hopewell believes that effective theological education would "pre-

---

50. *Ibid.*
51. Emery, *op. cit.,* p. 225.
52. Hopewell, "Preparing the Candidate for Mission," *Theological Education by Extension,* pp. 46-47.

suppose a system of continuous, developmental education that dogged a man throughout his life and capitalized upon his growing experience."[53] But that kind of education, which teaches men to wrest truth not only from the printed page, but from all of life's experiences is not overly stimulated by the passive teaching methodology so common in traditional theological education.

Dropout Percentage. The dropout rate in the ministry among men trained in traditional theological institutions is high. Furthermore, because of the high investment in each student and the embarrassing situation of sending home a student who claims to be called of God, once a student has begun his course of study ". . . there is a tendency to try and see him through his schooling regardless of whether or not he is a good student or has potential as a leader in the Church."[54] There exists the tendency to perpetuate the training of the unqualified for face-saving reasons.

Economic Costlines. Closely intertwined with all of the above looms the question of cost. Residence education is costly in current expenses and capital investment, and more so when there is a markedly low student-faculty ratio. Thus, full-time personnel who could easily serve more students simply do not have those students on their campus. Receipts from student fees are negligible and offerings from churches minimal, and the investment per student is extremely high. While the cost of educating a secondary student in residence at the Evangelical High School of San Pedro Sula, Honduras, was about $500 per year, it cost nearly $3,000 for each theological student in residence at the Theological Institute of the Evangelical and Reformed Church of Honduras, even though the institutions were across the street from each other and the students shared the same dormitories.

Is "the way we've always done it" the best approach? Does the traditional residence pattern we have so eagerly exported really fit the needs of Third World churches? Is that pattern genuinely biblical? Can traditional residence institutions possibly train the vast number of leaders required by a rapidly growing church? And can

---

53. *Ibid.,* p. 42.
54. Rowen, *op. cit.*

they produce the kind of quality leaders who are authentic representatives of their own people rather than pale shadows of their missionary teachers? These are serious questions every theological
educator, every missionary, every pastor and layman interested in the
church's worldwide mission needs to struggle with and draw his own
conclusions.

Chapter II

CONTEXT FOR CHANGE: THE LATIN AMERICAN REALITY

One of the factors influencing contemporary theological education in Latin America is the imported residence pattern. But it is not the only factor. Dr. Donald A. McGavran is correct when he adds: "Theological education around the world must fit the economic and educational standards of the population being evangelized."[1] In addition to these factors, I would stress the importance of anthropological analysis.

ANTHROPOLOGICALLY

Because the scope of this book is limited, the discussion of the anthropological reality of Latin America as it bears upon theological education will be limited primarily to a discussion of the presence of subcultures and indigenous leadership patterns. While this section focuses particularly on Guatemala, what is true there is true for most parts of Latin America, especially where a high percentage of the population are Indians.

The Presence of Subcultures

A classic example of anthropological analysis as it bears upon theological education appears in the article, "The Preparation of Leaders in a Ladino-Indian Church," by James Emery.[2] Faced with the problem of setting up a single program to train leaders for a church whose constituency includes a wide spectrum of sub-cultures,

---

1. Donald A. McGavran, "Foreword," *Theological Education by Extension,* pp. xiii-xv.
2. James Emery, "The Preparation of Leaders in a Ladino-Indian Church," *Practical Anthropology* X (1963), pp. 127-134.

Diagram B: Cultural Gradations in Guatemalan Communities

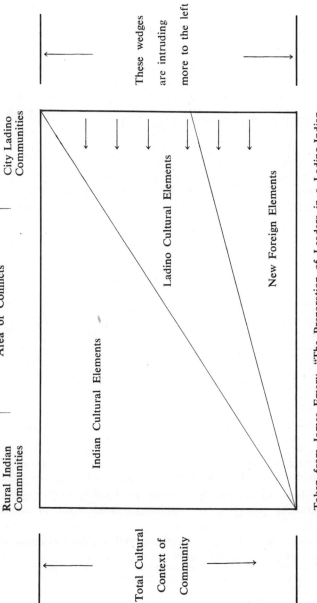

Rural Indian Communities

Area of Conflicts

City Ladino Communities

Indian Cultural Elements

Ladino Cultural Elements

New Foreign Elements

These wedges are intruding more to the left

Total Cultural Context of Community

Taken from James Emery, "The Preparation of Leaders in a Ladino-Indian Church," *Practical Anthropology* X (1963), p. 127.

Emery made a keen analysis of the anthropological reality existing within the Presbyterian Synod of Guatemala.

Within its rectangular boundaries in southwestern Guatemala, one finds steaming costal plains populated largely by rural Latin poor; the burgeoning capital city of Guatemala inhabited by educated professionals, a rising middle class, and urban poor; and the number two city, Quetzaltenango, perched atop an 8,000-foot plateau which is the center of the progressive Quiche Indian population and borders on the area inhabited by the isolated Mam Indians. These highland Indians wrest their living from tiny terraced plots carved like steps out of the steep highland hills, which they cultivate by hand. Many supplement their income by going down to the coastal coffee and banana plantations during that time of the year when their own land lies dormant. Emery has prepared a diagram to illustrate graphically the cultural reality of this area.[3] See Diagram B. This diagram illustrates the anthropological reality arising out of the dynamic interaction of the various subcultures, data which must be taken into account in setting up any leadership training program.

Guatemalan communities in the Presbyterian zone run the gamut from the almost completely Indian to the almost totally Spanish. Whenever one of the cultural elements finds itself in a small minority, it tends to cede to the dominant culture—albeit unwillingly at times—but where there are more equal proportions of Indians and Ladinos, there are many conflicts:

> This is the area of rapid acculturation where different values are being contested and it is in this type of situation the Presbyterian churches are located.[4]

Emery warns that cultural borrowing from the United States and Europe should not be underestimated. To the growing industrialization and the extensive road building program of the government, add the ingredient of marked instability to this scene of rapid social change—at least at the level of material culture; although attitudes, thought patterns, and customs tend to persist more tenaciously.

---

3. *Ibid.*, p. 128.
4. *Ibid.*, p. 127.

Traditional Leadership Patterns

One of the key insights of anthropology for theological education is to discern the leadership pattern present in a given subculture. Within the same cultural milieu, Emery mentions four patterns of leadership, while Nida and Wonderly discern five different authority systems at work within the Guatemalan Indian community.[5] Knowledge of the traditional pattern is of special importance for theological education. In most sectors of society, leaders have been trained while undertaking successive responsibilities. The training is concurrent with the job, and selection takes place as the person either advances to the next stage or is dropped.

While Emery does not always agree with Nida and Wonderly, they are in basic accord in delineating the basic characteristics of the traditional leadership system which is still extremely strong in most rural areas, especially those with a high Indian population. What are the characteristics of this system?

First, it is a "ladder" system in that it "presents a minute gradation; no one can reach a position of authority without having first passed through the lower positions and demonstrated his aptitude in them."[6]

Second, it is a representative system, although not necessarily democratic; the decisions of the elders are passively ratified by the whole group. Nevertheless "they are the most satisfactory type of decisions for the Indian community because they are made by men who have risen through the required steps and who are therefore considered as the legitimate representatives of their community."[7]

Third, it is an apprenticeship system. "The participants are not prepared by means of formal study, but begin as apprentices with a simple responsibility and climb from one position to another, preparing themselves in this way by means of the experience gained."[8] Emery adds:

---

5. Eugene A. Nida and William A. Wonderly, "Selection, Preparation, and Function of Leaders in Indian Fields," *Practical Anthropology* X (1963), pp. 7-16.

6. *Ibid.*, p. 8.   7. *Ibid.*   8. *Ibid.*

The training is concurrent with the job and selection is indicated as the person either advances to the next stage or else is dropped. . . . The same thing happens, however, in other areas of the culture and is the procedure in most trades. . . . The selecton is thus informal, but effective.[9]

Fourth, it is a system which places a premium on mature, older men, guaranteeing "that the positions of greater responsibility shall be occupied only by older men, who have previously gone through the lower positions."[10] It is interesting to note that in churches which follow this system of leadership preparation, although most ordained pastors are over 40, this has not alienated the youth. It may, in fact, be a source of identification with the youth in that the elder has passed through the same steps in which the youth are now walking. He has walked in the shoes of his followers.

Fifth, it is a system in which the real leaders may not be the overt leaders, inasmuch as many true leaders view the assumption of overt leadership positions as lack of humility or possible corruption. Thus,

The men who do accept positions of nominal leadership often turn out to be the most ineffective type, and the real leaders tell them how to run things, or manage to work around them and get things done.[11]

I saw this reality in operation in the rural village of Nueva Esperanza, located in the Department of Yoro, Honduras. Pepe, a young single nephew of Jesús, was sent for a ten-week intensive course of study sponsored by the Theological Institute in order to serve as the lay leader of his congregation. And indeed it was Pepe who directed the worship services, but it was Jesús, a respected, middle-aged, though very poor family man with a lovely wife and teenage children who decided if there would be services and when they would be. It was to his home that all visitors were immediately taken and introduced, and his opinion was always accepted by the group even when he did not preside at the congregational meetings. Yet there seemed

9. Emery, "The Preparation of Leaders in a Ladino-Indian Church," *Practical Anthropology* X (1963), p. 129.

10. Nida and Wonderly, *op. cit.*, p. 8.

11. *Ibid.*, p. 13.

to be no conflict or power struggle within the congregation. The real leadership pattern, though decidedly low profiile, was acceptable to all.

It is exceedingly clear that the traditional pattern of leadership training is in conflict with a Western society, which places a premium on formal education and youth. Education serves to accelerate the method of slow advancement and natural selection, for by attending school it is possible to begin at a higher rung on the ladder, although from there on the traditional system in a moderate form does take over.[12] Both traditional apprenticeship patterns and the contemporary trend toward recognition of leadership via formal education need to be taken into account.

> This is part of the church's dilemma in Indian work in Latin America today: how to prepare leaders (whether Indian or mestizo) who on the one hand can appreciate the Indian cultural background, guide their people in terms of it, and be recognized as leaders in the society; and who on the other hand can prepare the newer generation in the Indian Church to effectively participate in the national life to which they aspire, to relate themselves to the fellowship of the church on the national level, and to withstand the social and moral pressures brought upon them through their increasing and inevitable contacts with the world at large.[13]

ECONOMICALLY

Passing from the anthropological to the economic reality in Latin America, we find the word "poverty" written large across the continent. Whereas the economic reality in the United States might be diagrammed in the shape of a diamond with a small percentage of the very rich and the very poor at either end with the vast majority in the wide middle area, Latin America may be described as a triangle with a few very wealthy at the pinnacle followed by a middle class that includes a sixth of the population—the rest belonging to the lower classes.[14]

---

12. Emery, "The Preparation of Leaders in a Ladino-Indian Church," *Practical Anthropology* X (1963), p. 129.

13. Nida and Wonderly, *op. cit.,* p. 13.

14. Information received at a consultation of the Commission on Society Development, and Peace (SODEPAX) sponsored by the World Council of Churches and the Papal Commission on Social Justice, held in San José, Costa

The per-capita income in United States dollars for the Latin American nations in 1967, according to the 1975 World Almanac, was as follows: Argentina, 1,138; Bolivia, 234; Brazil, 452; Colombia, 328; Costa Rica, 579; Cuba, 410; Chile, 796; Ecuador, 260; El Salvador, 304; Guatemala, 365; Haite, 90; Honduras, 268; Mexico, 717; Nicaragua, 463; Panama, 804; Paraguay, 273; Peru, 493; Republica Dominicana, 404; Uruguay, 686; Venezuela, 1,010.[15] Compared with these figures, France has a per-capita income of $3,824, West Germany of $4,219, Canada of $4,742, and the United States of $5,550. See diagram C.[16]

Those who believe that "living is cheap" in these Latin American nations need to be aware that it generally costs the United States government more to maintain its personnel on an equivalent standard of living in many of these Latin American countries than it costs to maintain them in Washington, D. C. The recent inflation-recession crunch has aggravated the problem and widened the gap between rich and poor. Inflation rates of 30% a year are not uncommon and in some countries have reached not two-digit, but three-digit figures annually. Poverty is both real and omnipresent in the Third World. This deeply affects theological education in that part of the world both for the ministerial candidate and for the training institution.

For the candidate, the economic factor, generally speaking, eliminates all but the very young without responsibility or the very wealthy with leisure. Full-time study beyond childhood years is very difficult. Lack of parental saving, an unemployment rate which usually hovers over 20%, and the difficulty of obtaining part-time work at any but infinitesimal wages, combine to make this a sad reality. Even if the prospective student is married, his wife, unless she is a professional,

---

Rica, during October, 1970. It is estimated that 2% of the population in Central America belongs to the upper classes, 18% to the middle class, and the remaining 80% to the lower classes. However, it is important to note that a solidly middle class high school principal probably earns no more than $250 to $350 per month.

15. María E. Alvarez del Real, directora, *1975 Almanaque Mundial* (Republic of Panama: Editorial America, S.A.), pp. 112-279. These figures are based on sources from the Population Reference Bureau. Per capita income is calculated by dividing the gross national product by the gross population.

16. *Ibid.*

Diagram C: Per Capita Income in Dollars for 1975 in Selected Areas

Selected Nations

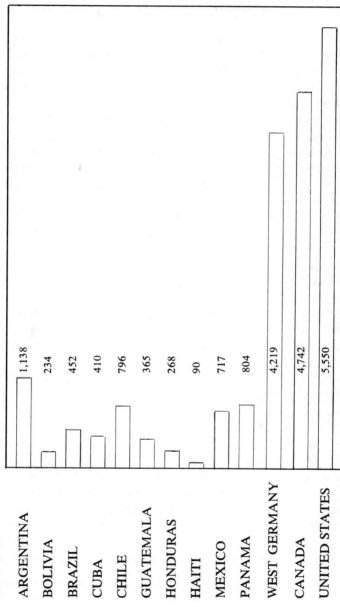

i.e., teacher, nurse, etc., cannot hope to earn sufficient money to support them. Many times cultural expectations demand that the one person in a large family who is earning money support those relatives who are out of work, even if all have to live on a subsistence level. These factors converge to make full-time residence study an impossible luxury for the majority of people unless they come either from the wealthy class or are single without family responsibility.

Also, the economic factor makes it unlikely that all but a few congregations can adequately support a full-time professional pastor, such as the traditional training institutions seem intent upon preparing. Emery notes that among the Presbyterians of Guatemala only 20 out of 71 congregations can afford full-time pastors and that in many of these instances the standard of living offered by the congregations is extremely low.[17] Many national leaders are trained beyond the capacity of the church to support them and for many churches, the inability to support a full-time professional pastor means no trained leadership at all.[18]

Finally, the economic reality of Latin America means that the pastor will receive a low economic return for the time invested in his education. Christian LaLive d'Epinay notes that the comparative rarity of vocations among the Protestant community as compared with the Pentecostal community in Chile is ". . . due primarily to the discrepancy between the theological requirements and the ridiculously low level of salaries."[19]

Three years of full-time study on a secondary or university level inevitably brings a greater financial remuneration to the student than three years invested in a theological training institution. The graduate of a secondary school can be well on his way to being a doctor or lawyer instead of a pastor, and a woman a nurse instead of a Christian education director or Bible woman. Even a primary school graduate can be on his way to being an accountant or skilled craftsman which

17. Emery, "The Preparation of Leaders in a Ladino-Indian Church," *Practical Anthropology* X (1963), pp. 130-31.
18. Rowen, *op. cit.,* cf. Stuart I. Troutman, "Theological Education in Central America," p. 8. Unpublished manuscript.
19. LaLive d'Epinay, *op. cit.,* p. 188.

will pay him materially better than the pastorate.

While the idealistic young student may overlook this, often his parents do not. Since adequate social security and welfare systems are practically non-existent for much of the population in Latin America, parents look to their children as their old-age insurance. They sacrifice to advance the child (especially elder sons) not only for his good, but also for their own security. The pastorate provides very little economic security.

The struggle of Andrés is enlightening. Andrés had a scholarship to attend the evangelical high school in San Pedro Sula. There he proved to be an outstanding student and leader. He graduated with a primary teaching certificate and was appointed to a position in the parochial school system of the church, but he felt called to the pastorate. His father, a lay preacher, is very poor and has sacrificed greatly for his son. Although Andrés would receive a full scholarship to cover his seminary expenses, his father would remain in poverty. To complicate the matter the government, also recognizing the ability of Andrés, had offered him a three-year scholarship to study education at university level. To begin his teaching career immediately would mean a starting salary of $100 a month; to finish the university course would guarantee a starting salary of $200 a month; to attend seminary would lead to a beginning salary of only $60 a month upon graduation. Andrés was troubled. It was not only a matter of the future long-term help that he could give his parents through a more lucrative teaching position, but the fact that he was already past 21. For years he had received and received and received what little his parents could afford and had never been able to repay anything. To attend seminary meant three more years of the same pattern. It was only at his father's strong urging that he went ahead to begin seminary studies.

The economic reality in the Latin American sector of the Third World creates problems not only for the individual ministerial candidate, but for the institution as well. Institutional finances are not unlimited. Most theological training institutions would like to move toward self-support, but theological education is expensive, and small student bodies (the average student body in Latin American seminaries is 27) means high per-student investment. Students who must be supported by scholarships because they come from poor families and cannot secure part-time work place an increased burden on the institution. Even a scholarship which includes not only tuition but also room and board does not necessarily solve the problem completely for students with dependent parents or siblings. For instance, a primary school teacher who wanted to study Christian education was not able to do so even though she was offered a scholarship, because she was the sole means of support for her aged parents. Most training schools are simply not in a position to give grants to the parents of the students as well as to the students themselves!

EDUCATIONALLY

Still another factor which bears upon theological education is the Latin American educational pattern. There is little doubt that the North American pattern of formal education concentrated in one's youth, coupled with the increasing tendency toward specialization, is gaining ground in Latin America. Nevertheless, the fact remains that only a tiny percentage of Latin Americans are privileged to receive a high school or university education.

Patterns of Adult Education

Although the masses cannot study full-time, there is a hunger for education. Thus, university, secondary, and even primary education in some cases, is increasingly taking on the following characteristics:

First, it is part-time study. Part-time study in the evening over a long period of time is becoming a part of life of increasing numbers of people. Both government and private schools offer primary and secondary education at night although in most cases a person can complete only a single grade a year due to the inclusion of minor courses and the use of the same educational methodology with adults as employed to teach children. At the University of Costa Rica, which enrolls 20,000 students, it takes the average university student eight to ten years to finish his course of study.

Second, it is evening study. This is due to the fact that most students work during the day and attend classes in the evening. The evangelical Mariano Galvez Uuiversity of Guatemala limits itself strictly to an evening program, as does the University of Honduras in San Pedro Sula. However, a viable alternative employed by many universities is early morning study. Indeed, numerous universities have few or no classes between 10:00 a.m. and 3:00 p.m.

Third, the tendency toward part-time evening study is reflected in the formation of a part-time evening faculty. Many doctors, lawyers, dentists, engineers, government workers, businessmen, and accountants serve as professors after office hours. For many, teaching is an avocation, as well as a means for supplementing the family income. While this does tend to inject a practical flavor into the educational process, it can also result in lack of preparation, faculty absenteeism, and indifference toward students.

Pedagogical Development

The part-time, evening pattern of adult education in Latin America, when coupled with significant recent breakthroughs in pedagogy, opens the door to possibilities for new approaches in theological education. Three of these recent emphases have been very significant.

Learning through Active Participation. The first of these is the growing awareness that the best learning takes place when the learner is actively involved as a participant in the learning process. While we remember only 10% of what we hear and 30% of what we see, we remember 90% of what we do. Therefore, modern pedagogy places great emphasis upon guided inductive study, which focuses not only on giving information to the student, but also on teaching him how to come to his own conclusions on the basis of evidence he has dug out for himself. Retention is better, and the student is much better equipped to continue learning on his own after leaving the institution than if he receives spoon-fed information to be retained by rote.

The recent development of self-study materials for theological education makes such an emphasis not only theoretically correct, but immensely practical. Not only can standard theological texts be adapted to the academic level and cultural background of the student through the use of workbooks, but the insistence on working systematically toward reaching measurable goals in appropriate steps (that goes with programmed instruction) holds genuine promise for the renovation of teaching methodology.[20] Such materials require constant, immediate response to the course content by the student in order to underscore the important, explain the obscure, evaluate, interpret, and apply. The course content can be organized in its most logical form so that the learning process is progressive and leads to significant comprehension. Because the basic course content and outline are determined by the materials instead of being dependent on the teacher, he has more time to develop other aspects of the course in an interesting and creative way rather than use his time in the basic gathering and organization of materials.

Self-study materials require the student to apply himself constantly throughout a course—not just when it comes time to write a report or take an examination. The student becomes an active participant in the education process as he reacts, decides, and evaluates at each step. As he applies himself more outside of class, he has a better basis upon which to participate while in class. And as the student learns to study and think by himself, he is training himself to continue studying after he graduates.

While many theological educators have a preconceived "negative attitude toward workbooks as 'for children' or 'for correspondence courses,' they are used extensively at the best universities and technical schools in other fields, such as physics, engineering, chemistry, etc."[21] Furthermore, while "self-study materials are essential to extension programs where the teacher-student contact is limited, they hold the same values for more traditional programs."[22] I can vouch for the accuracy of the last statement, for I have used self-study materials, or directed-study materials as they are sometimes called, in both residence and extension programs with equally positive results.

---

20. Wayne C. Weld, *The World Dictionary of Theological Education by Extension* (South Pasadena, Calif.: William Carey Library, 1973), p. 27.
21. F. Ross Kinsler, "The Importance and Advantages of Self-Study Materials in Theological Education," *The Extension Seminary and the Programmed Textbook—the report of a workshop*, pp. 27-28.
22. *Ibid.*, p. 27.

In short, constant active participation in the learning process by the theological student has been made possible through the development of self-study materials in workbook or programmed format. By means of such prepared materials—

> . . . the best teachers in the field can be brought to the most isolated institution, and any number of institutions can cooperate in order to produce the best possible materials. . . . The materials can provide a constant application and practical orientation of the course content to the life and ministry of the student in his own particular situation. . . . The materials themselves, and thus the educational process, can be constantly evaluated and improved—something difficult to achieve in the traditional, teacher-dominated methods.[23]

The "Split Rail Fence" Analogy. A second emphasis of special importance has to do with the development of the "split rail fence" as a viable educational analogy for professional education. Dr. Ted Ward, professor at the Institute for International Studies at Michigan State University, notes that current curriculum developments for professional education constitute an observable trend, provide a common base, and reflect three characteristics: "a) increasing use of field experiences, b) more variety in approach as to cognitive learning, and c) greater articulation between field experience and cognitive learning through seminars, symposia, and other forms of shared experiences."[24] Ward illustrates these characteristics with a metaphor from days gone by, ". . . namely that frontier artifact of the split rail fence."[25] See Diagram D. The upper rail represents the cognitive input; the lower rail represents field experiences; and the fence posts represent the seminars which serve as small-group linkages between cognitive input and field experience. Ward continues:

In the rail fence there are two sets of variables that determine

---

23. *Ibid.*
24. Ted Ward, "The Split-Rail Fence: An Analogy for the Education of professionals," *The Extension Seminary* I, no. 2, p. 4. This material appears in a more polished form as part of an article co-authored by Ward and Samuel F. Rowen, "The Significance of the Extension Seminary," *Evangelical Missions Quarterly* IX, No. 1 (Fall, 1972), pp. 17-27.
25. *Ibid.*

Diagram D: The Split Rail Fence Analogy for Professional Education

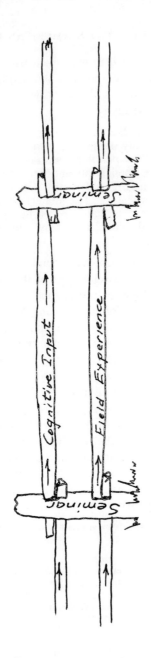

The Upper Rail   Cognitive Input

The Lower Rail: Field Experience

The Fenceposts: Seminars

Taken from Ted Ward, "The Split-Rail Fence: Analogy for Professional Education," *Extension Seminary*, no. 2, p. 5.

the selection of design characteristics: the use or function of the fence, and the balance of the components. With reference to the former, a fence is "good," if it performs a designated function over a stipulated period of time. A decorative fence does not need to be strong enough to contain cattle, but a cattle fence may or may not also need to be decorative; in any case, the fence's life span in relation to its cost is an important consideration. With reference to the second set of variables, balance, the chief proposition here is that a fence's components, like those of a chain, need to be selected or designed for strength. The "weakest link" principle pertains; a fence is not made "better" by increasing the size of the upper rail (unless, of course, that had been the "weakest link"); conversely, to decrease the substance of the posts weakens the entire system.[26]

After further illustrating the relation of the two variables. function and balance, to each other, Ward turns to definition and exposition of exactly what he means by the different components of his split rail fence metaphor.

First, he defines cognitive input—the upper rail.

"Cognitive input" refers to the learning of the knowledge needed for competence and excellence. What is cognitive (knowable as information) ranges from simple concrete facts up through abstract concepts and problem solving strategies. Cognitive input, in a sense, concerns the "things to be learned"; but it would be more useful to think of cognitive input as the *information that can be learned by reading, hearing, or looking.* Cognitive input is provided through a wide variety of instructional modes: through textbooks, assigned readings, lectures, recordings, film and programmed instruction of several sorts. "New media" of instruction are sometimes employed so that the cognitive input can be more effective or effcient.[27]

"Unfortunately," continues Ward, "it is often the cognitive input component that is particularly prone to problems toward low learner motivation and rapid content obsolescence. A curriculum that overemphasizes cognitive input is likely to be characterized by high

---

26. *Ibid.,* p. 5.
27. *Ibid.*

drop-out rates and frequent student complaints about irrelevancy."[28]

Second, Ward defines field experiences—the lower rail—as "exposure to the environment and 'life problems' of the practitioner during the period of formal educational experience."[29] He sees getting experience "where the action is," such as takes place in modern medical education, as one useful answer for the demand that education be relevant.

> Recognition of the validity of field experience has also had a remarkable effect on the concept of in-service education (sometimes called "continuing education," to denote its life-long characteristic). The older and simpler practice of transplanting the campus-oriented course to some remote point, lock, stock, and barrel—syllabus, text, and professor—is disappearing. The modern extension and continuing education operation capitalizes on the fact that in-service professionals are engaged in experiences, day by day, that constitute a rich source of material for evaluation, reconsideration and in sum, for valuable learning. When extension education makes effective use of the field experiences that confront the in-service practitioner, it is a worthy competitor to the more formal and classical forms of graduate education, and is certainly a great improvement over the "transplanted course" approach.[30]

Third, it is the seminars or fence posts that make the connection between cognitive input and field experience.

> Something exciting happens when learners get together to put into *words* how new information is related to their doing an effective job. If left to chance or individual initiative, new information may never result in appropriate changes in the professional practice, or worse yet, it will result in incorrect application to practice. Misunderstandings in the cognitive realm can result in disasters in the realm of practice. The seminar as an opportunity for reflecting, evaluating, and hypothesizing, can reduce the gaps and misapplications, resulting in more potent and responsible transfers from "theory" to "practice" and back again to theory.[31]

Although "seminar" is one of those words which often escape precise

---

28. *Ibid.*, pp. 5-6.   29. *Ibid.*, p. 6.   30. *Ibid.*   31. *Ibid.*

definition, Ward uses it to indicate the less structured sharing and discussion experiences. According to him:

> The hallmarks of a good seminar are the occasions and stimulations to reflect upon and evaluate learning from both the cognitive input and from the field experiences, with a premium on relating the two. The objectives of a seminar can usually be expressed in terms of applying principles and concepts to problem-solving tasks.[32]

So the analogy of the split-rail fence, "two lines of parallel linear flow, supported and integrated by spaced interpractice seminars," has provided theological educators with an idealized model for pastoral and leadership training.[33]

A Critique of Traditional Schooling

A third development, the impact of which has not yet been fully felt by theological educators as the previous two breakthroughs, is the radical critique of traditional schooling, theological and otherwise, usually associated with the names of Ivan Illich and Paulo Freire. Wagner goes so far as to warn: "One can only hope that evangelical Christianity will not run quite so far behind Ivan Illich and Paulo Freire as it did behind Copernicus and Galileo."[34]

Most schools in Latin America are overcrowded and under-equipped. Pre-packaged academic programs are usually laid out at distant government offices without taking into account the needs of the student. Subject matter is delivered through copy and recite methods at the primary level and through lectures and examinations at the secondary and university levels. Minimal attention is given to investigation and experimentation. The result is the loss of natural curiosity and motivation with the corresponding introduction of artificial stimuli and discipline in the form of threats and grades.

And yet education—this kind of schooling aimed at the rote accumulation of knowledge for future use—is the key to upward social

---

32. *Ibid.*, p. 7.
33. *Ibid.*
34. C. Peter Wagner, "Seminaries Ought to Be Asking Who as Well as How," *Theological Education* X (Summer, 1974), p. 266.

and economic mobility not only in Latin America, but in most of the Third World.

Faced with the increasing demand for education, the typical government response—looking to the United States as a model for their public education—is to require more compulsory education and multiply the number of schools. First elementary school is the norm, then high school, then university, then graduate school. And the cost? Staggering! While the United States may be wealthy enough to support a system of near universal schooling up through the university level, the inflation-eroded economies of many Latin American nations can maintain such a system for only a relatively small segment of the population. It is physically impossible to enroll anywhere near all the prospective students in the limited facilities available. Education remains aristocratic. But in the attempt to enroll as many as possible, the schools remain overcrowded and underequipped with devastating results on the quality of education.

Illich, an Austrian-born ex-Catholic priest who spent many years in parish work in the United States before establishing himself in Cuernavaca, Mexico, is best known for his radical ideas on "deschooling."[35] Freire, a Brazilian educator, has developed a methodology and philosophy called conscientization, or consciousness-raising. He has worked out his concepts primarily in relation to adult education, more specifically literacy. He begins with the student, entering into dialogue in order to learn with him about his world. He has discovered that as the person reflects upon his problems, faces them, and takes action to solve them, he more truly realizes his human potential. Although both Illich and Freire are dealing with different aspects of the problem and are often at variance, they do, nevertheless, agree on several basic thrusts in their search for educational alternatives.

First, both demand that living, learning, and working be interconnected and contextual. They flatly deny that learning is a direct result of teaching and that learning and schooling are co-terminous. Illich baldly states: "We have all learned most of what we know

---

35. Ivan Illich, *Deschooling Society* (New York: Harper & Row, Publishers, 1970). Illich defines as ". . . the age-specific, teacher-related, process requiring full-time attendance at an obligatory curriculum," p. 38.

outside of school."[36] They attempt to show how persons learn more outside of school than in school.

Second, both believe that education must start with the needs of the student. They strike at the nerve center of institution-centered education. Wagner stresses the importance of this insight for theological education when he criticizes the tendency to conform the incoming student to fit the institution instead of conforming the institution to fit the needs of the gifted person whom God has raised up as leader of his church.

Third, both Illich and Freire believe that both students and teachers have something to contribute to the learning process. No one teaches anyone; rather people learn together in a real world, insists Freire.[37] This kind of adult education opens the door for quality education experiences which involve a sharing of wisdom not only from textbooks, but from the stuff of everyday life and ministry. Freire's premise that a student's own memory forms the basis for teaching can infuse new life into theological education.

The writings of Illich and Freire, coupled with the developing interest in non-formal education and the creation of new open universities hold immense promise for the transformation of ministerial training in Latin America.[38]

---

36. *Ibid.*, p. 42.

37. Paulo Freire, *Educación Liberadora* (Medellín: Editorial Prisma, 1972), pp. 22-35. Cf. *Pedagogía del Oprimido* (Montevideo: Tierra Nueva, 1970), pp. 75-99; *La Educación como Práctica de la Libertad* (México: Siglo Veintiuno, 1972). For an incisive critique of Freire's idea of consciousness-raising, cf. Peter L. Berger, "The False Consciousness of 'Consciousness Raising,'" *Pyramids of Sacrifice: Political Ethics and Social Change* (New York: Basic Books, Inc., 1974).

38. "Descriptive analyses point out intriguing contrasts between formal and non-formal education. The tendency of formal school programs is to depend upon motivation within the content, have poor clarity of objectives, experience a low level of appropriate instructional technology, base validation on tradition, and offer symbolic rewards. The tendency of non-formal programs, on the other hand, is to find motivation within the learner, have a higher clarity of objectives, experience a high level of appropriate instructional technology, base validation on performance and application, and offer pragmatic rewards. . . . Non-formal education enables people to meet their needs and to do their jobs more effectively." F. Ross Kinsler, "Extension: An Alternative Model

After all, the whole Christian movement began not in a school, but with twelve laymen lacking in formal training—and a Master in the field of adult education.

for Theological Education," *Extension Seminary*, 1973:3, p. 6. Kinsler's methodology and content of theological education to contextualization, conscientization, and liberation are three basic concerns of development and education in general in Latin America today. Cf. Jaime Emery, "Educación no formal y los seminarios," *Alternative in la Educación Teológica* (San José, Costa Rica: Seminario Bíblico Latinamericano, 1975), pp. 33-34.

Chapter III

A NEW LOOK DOWN OTHER PATHS:
SOME VIABLE OPTIONS

While few theological educators are crying for the total abolition of the present residence system of theological training, many are declaring that traditional theological education must be supplemented, transformed, even eclipsed as the norm if the Protestant Church in Latin America is to be equipped to accomplish the work of ministry.

The history of theological education, biblical-theological guidelines, and an awareness of the multiform nature of the Latin American reality provide clues for the construction of models which may prove to be viable options. Several of these models are now in operation. Many are not new. They have simply been overlooked. Some reveal great promise; others grave deficiencies. Historically, they have been used both in isolation and combination with each other and with traditional theological education. They include correspondence courses, short-term institutes, evening Bible schools, apprenticeship, and extension.

CORRESPONDENCE

Many groups use correspondence courses to reach those who cannot study in residence programs. Books and materials are mailed to those who request them. Students fill out lessons and examinations and mail them to the sponsoring group, which in turn grades the examinations and returns the corrected paper to the student. This usually takes a minimum of two weeks—often much longer.

Some Protestant radio stations carry programs consisting of lectures and/or discussions co-ordinated with the lessons of a particular correspondence course. HCJB in Quito, Ecuador, founded the

55

"Christian Academy of the Air" in 1948 and has since prepared correspondence materials for an entire theological curriculum at secondary level. Their students number in the thousands. A diploma is awarded to graduates.

The Latin American Biblical Seminary in San José, Costa Rica, also produces a well-known correspondence course, which has been gradually upgraded.[1] Before upgrading, it consisted of a dozen courses, each with a text, divided into ten or twelve lessons per subject. By completing a lesson a week, a student could receive his diploma in about three years. In Honduras, it has been used extensively among leaders of the Evangelical and Reformed Church who were literate but had never completed more than a few grades of primary school. Correspondence study was supplemented by a month of residence study each year. However, the materials, though now much improved and upgraded, are not now usable for this purpose. They are too difficult.

Extremely simple courses are abundant. They are generally offered through evangelical radio programs. Quality varies markedly from course to course. Numerous evangelical homes throughout Latin America have certificates awarded upon completion of correspondence courses hanging on the walls. I have noted that many times such simple correspondence courses have served to arouse believers to further study. The cost to the student for knowledge gained is low.

Nevertheless, despite their value, correspondence courses have serious drawbacks as a major vehicle to carry out theological education in Latin America.

First, delayed feedback is unavoidable. Ward notes, "Short-term

---

1. I vividly recall a Baptist pastor whom I met in the jungles of Costa Rica. In addition to a few years of primary school, the only academic perparation for the congregation he pastored was the correspondence course which he had completed. The diploma which he had received from the Latin American Biblical Seminary hung front and center in the living room of his humble three room unpainted shack. The books and booklets he had received through the course comprised about 80% of his meager library. He carefully kept in his wallet the twelve cards which indicated satisfactory completion of each of the units in the total course.

courses on campus have the advantage of an instructor immediately available. Extension courses, likewise. Correspondence courses— none at all. By the time the instructor scribbles the remarks across the page and mails it back it has gone stale. One of the things we know about human learning is that the person while engaged in learning activity needs a lot of feedback" which cannot be provided by a correspondence course.[2]

Second, extremely high motivation is demanded. The lack of personal contact due to an absentee instructor often means that motivation is low. Low motivation leads to a high dropout rate. While Ward admits that many "correspondence course operations depend for their financial security on dropouts," he also adds, "If you can't design your screening processes any better than to have a 40% dropout rate, something is wrong."[3]

Third, updating is costly. Correspondence courses of any quality are so expensive to produce because of their specialized nature that they cannot be constantly updated. It is not unusual for the same material to be in use ten or more years.

Fourth, immediate relevancy is difficult to obtain. Thinking again of the analogy of the split rail fence, cognitive input through correspondence courses may be high—in fact, the student has to struggle on his own; but supervised field experience is nil, and scribbled comments from an absentee instructor are a poor substitute for a seminar experience. Furthermore, precisely because many materials are translated from English without being subjected to cultural adaptation, and make their way into a wide variety of subcultures, their specific relevancy to any given situation is often very low.

In summary, correspondence courses are at best supplemental and peripheral means of theological education, although they may be of marked value and benefit to the highly motivated student. Standing alone, they cannot be taken as a serious alternative to traditional theological education.

---

2. Ted Ward, "Programmed Learning Techniques," *Theological Education by Extension*, p. 313.
3. *Ibid.*, p. 316.

SHORT TERM INSTITUTES

Short term institutes are concentrated courses of leadership training which generally last anywhere from two weeks to three months. They are commonly used for the training of rural church leadership because they do not uproot the student from his environment. Generally, they are spaced during the year to fall at times when farming activity is minimal in the rural areas. While they may be held in a centrally located city, they are often held at whatever primitive facilities the host church in a given region can provide—unless, of course, there is a conveniently located mission compound!

Under some circumstances, the short term institute becomes a workable option for serious theological education, for instance, in the polished form which the Assemblies of God have adopted in Latin America and elsewhere in the world. In apparent conscious acceptance of the dictum expressed by Winter, "The best pastor to a given group is almost always someone from that particular culture. . . ."[4] They employ a pattern of one semester—four months—of residence study per year for a minimum of six years.

Generally speaking, the student is already the leader of a given congregation which has assumed responsibility for the support of the candidate's family and the ministry of the local church during his absence. However, if the institute is close enough he may return on weekends to assume pastoral responsibilities. At the Assembly's Bible Institute in San Pedro Sula, Honduras, the minimal level for matriculation was a third-grade education, although sometimes exception was made in the case of literate natural leaders with innate intelligence.

The entire institute program for adult Christian education is standardized throughout the continent. It includes syllabus, texts, and teaching methods—all outlined and packaged in a valuable binder.

Serious effort is made to teach the student how to study, and the

---

4. Ralph D. Winter, "Cultural Distance and Ministerial Training," *The Extension Seminary and the Programmed Textbook—a report on a workshop,* p. 9.

latest educational methodology is employed in the production of teaching materials, i.e., texts, workbooks, audio-visuals, etc.

Attendance in consecutive years is not required, but a student must complete six semesters of study successfully by attending every other year, and some take up to a dozen years to complete their education. Often the facilities are used year-round by following the four-month semester for men by a four-month semester for women, followed by four months of use for youth conferences, conventions, and other denominational gatherings. Students attend classes in the morning. After supervised study in the early afternoon, they work on the grounds and in the kitchen to keep costs low. Weekends are generally devoted to pastoral and evangelistic work.

Such a program does have noticeable advantages. It avoids cultural dislocation; the student does not tear up roots in his community. The students are usually already leaders in their congregations. The local churches assume clearly defined responsibility. The students are not forced to assimilate more in a four-month period than they can put into practice during the next eight months.

But on the other hand, the program all but eliminates those urban tent-making pastors who cannot leave their jobs for a four-month period each year. Emphasis on indoctrination is very strong, and this can lead to the student's becoming a passive receptacle for sound doctrine. The academic level is extremely low. The standardized program appears somewhat wooden, stilted, and rigid, although some allowance is made for flexibility, and creativity is verbally encouraged. North American influence also seems quite strong.

Nevertheless, the short-term institute in the form used by various Pentecostal groups shows promise in some areas and among some peoples as being a truly viable option for leadership training in Latin America.

EVENING BIBLE SCHOOLS

In his significant article, "Training a Tent-Making Ministry in Latin America," James F. Hopewell, director of the Theological Education Fund between 1965 and 1970, notes that one of the genuine contributions of the churches of the Third World to the worldwide body of Christ is their "valuable experience in educating ordinands to assume . . . ministries . . . which require a presbyter to maintain a secular occupation."[5]

The vast majority of the more than 75,000 functioning Pentecostal pastors in Latin America work at least part-time in some secular pursuit. How can they be trained? Hopewell states the issue acutely:

> It is increasingly apparent that any large numbers of "tent-making" ministers cannot be trained by traditional methods of theological education. Private study and apprenticeship schemes, on the one hand tend to be haphazard and atomized affairs. To take, on the other hand, any quantity of mature men through the normal three to five-year residence course in a theological school and support their families, would be a luxury that most churches in the world could not affortd. The traditional residence course has other disadvantages. Should a man already established in a secular profession (a characteristic which may mark the most promising of candidates for tent-making ministries) be removed by this long period in seminary from the very occupation he would resume after graduation? Re-entry is often difficult, and he would learn his theology away from the immediate context of his secular career. And will persons who enjoy their secular work (another characteristic) be recruited to a three-to-five year vacation from it?[6]

Hopewell sees the evening Bible school as a possible alternative to either private study or the traditional course taken in residence. These schools are low level training institutions with emphasis on the mastery of the content of the Bible in the vernacular. Strong emphasis is placed on practical courses, often taught very mechanically. The Theological Education Fund now estimates that there are an estimated 300 such Bible schools in existence in Latin America, about five for every regular theological school. An evening Bible school is simply a Bible school which limits its program to study in the evening. In addition to their usual concern for conservative theology, Hopewell notes that Latin American evening Bible schools have other significant characteristics:

---

5. James F. Hopewell, "Training a Tent-Making Ministry in Latin America," *International Review of Missions* LV (1966), p. 333.

6. *Ibid.,* pp. 333-334.

They are more prevalent in churches experiencing rapid expansion. . . . Bible schools frequently enjoy a distinctly higher proportion of local financial support for their operation than do traditional Seminaries in Latin America. . . . They lead a more independent life than do other seminaries. . . . Requirements for entrance do not usually require any pledge regarding ordination nor do they include a particular scholastic attainment. It is not unusual to find mechanics, lawyers, shop clerks and teachers in a single class. . . . Enrollments are high, often over one hundred. . . . Regular attendance is higher than might be imagined. . . . the schools usually operate with the disapproval of the "higher" seminaries, even those of the same denomination. . . . The list of courses taught reads like most seminary catalogues. Classes usually consist of lectures. Outside reading may be encouraged, but not always expected. Examinations are the rule, and, at the end of the course, an impressive diploma is awarded. The quality of teaching, while not spectacular, is not necessarily inadequate.[7]

From Hopewell's description and analysis of the evening Bible schools, three principles can be cited for their success:

First, these schools manage to teach theology to people who have secular occupations mainly by operating where and when working people have free time.

Second, these schools attract and retain so many students under conditions that might be thought intolerable because they have followed the widely accepted pattern of part-time evening study prevalent in Latin America, so that Bible school students feel themselves part of that massive movement of men seeking education in spare moments.

Third, there is an atmosphere of sacrificial dedication that pervades the schools: ". . . an electric spirit . . . an atmosphere that shouts that these are the best hours of the day and that these hours are being used, in God's sight, to the best possible advantages."[8]

APPRENTICESHIP TRAINING

Theological education through apprenticeship, once the norm in many parts of the United States, is presently found in its purest form

7. *Ibid.*, pp. 334-336.
8. *Ibid.*, p. 336.

among the Chilean Pentecostals, and it exists to varying degrees among other groups in Latin America.

In 1965, Christian LaLive d'Epinay, an assistant in sociology at the University of Geneva, was engaged by the Department of Mission Studies of the World Council of Churches to do research among the Pentecostals of Chile under the auspices of an organization called Church and Society in Latin America (ISAL). In addition to publishing the results of his monumental study under the title *Refuge of the Masses,* he also published shorter articles indicating the results of his research. One of these is "The Training of Pastors and Theological Education: The Case of Chile."[9]

In this article he delineates and explains the Pentecostal apprenticeship system in the total context of Protestant theological education in Chile, especially taking into account the Methodists and Presbyterians who were then committed to the traditional system.

> It has become commonplace to stress the lack of theological education (in fact, of any education at all) of the Pentecostalist leaders. Far less often is attention drawn to the high level of theological education among the Methodist or Presbyterian pastors and the complete stagnation of those denominations! Without claiming that there may be a *causal* relationship between the theological level of the pastors and the evangelistic dynamism of their denominations, the existence of correlation between these two facts makes us less confident of the benefits of theological education in the developed countries which we impose on Protestants in the developing nations. . . . Who should teach whom?[10]

The statistical difference between the average Pentecostal pastor and the average Protestant pastor is even more astounding. The former is over 40, has a primary education or less, and is a convert. The latter is under 40, has had some university study in addition to his theological studies, and was born in a Protestant home.[11]

LaLive concludes that "these basic differences are not due to chance, but are directly connected with the pastoral training system which itself is one of the main factors in determining the structural

---

9. LaLive d'Epinay, *op. cit.,* pp. 185-192.
10. *Ibid.,* p. 185.
11. *Ibid.,* pp. 187-196.

specifics of Protestantism on the one hand and of Pentecostalism on the other."[12]

"Whereas Protestant pastors are 'trained by the seminary,' Pentecostalist pastors are 'trained by the street.' "[13] The Pentecostalists themselves use the latter expression indicating that they serve their apprenticeship through assisting in the corporate evangelization effort of their own congregation, which generally begins in the streets. At the same time they remain with their families, work at their jobs, and maintain their normal social contacts.[14]

With keen discernment, LaLive notes two crucial characteristics of the Pentecostal system. First, every convert is an evangelist. Second, every convert can one day be entrusted with pastoral responsibilties if he has the gifts or qualities of a preacher and leader.

However, to attain the pastoral office takes time. The beginner has to climb the rungs of the hierarchical ladder one by one. Wagner identifies seven rungs in the ladder: street preacher, Sunday school teacher, preacher, founder of a new preaching point, officially recognized "worker for the Lord," pastor-deacon, pastor.[15] LaLive describes the process in depth:

> Soon after his conversion he starts as a preacher in the street, where he proves the depth of his convictions and the quality of his witness. He will then be given responsibilities for a Sunday school class and will accede to the status of preacher; he will then have the right to lead worship. If he gives satisfaction, his pastor may entrust him to the task of opening a new preaching place in his neighborhood. . . . Here for the first time the believer can demonstrate his charisma. If he succeeds in gathering a small group the elders and the pastor will regard this as adequate proof of his vocation, because they are convinced that it is not man who converts, but the power of God within him; a vocation which does not bear fruit cannot be of God.[16]

---

12. *Ibid.,* p. 187.
13. *Ibid.,* p. 188.
14. Pedro Wagner, *¡Cuidado! Ahí vienen los Pentecostales!* Benjamin E. Mercado, trans. (Miami: Editorial Vida, 1973), p. 107. Cf. Ralph R. Covell and C. Peter Wagner, *An Extension Seminary Primer* (South Pasadena, Calif.: William Carey Library), pp. 62-69.
15. *Ibid.,* pp. 108-110.
16. LaLive d'Epinay, *op. cit.,* p. 189.

It is only after the candidate has reached this state, which may take years, that he can tell his pastor that he feels called to the ministry. At the Annual Conference he will be proposed as a "worker for the Lord." If approved he will be sent to work in a new area to prove once more that God is working through him by building up a new congregation. If he succeeds in gathering a congregation, he will probably be appointed as a pastor deacon, which is the first pastoral grade. But if he fails, he returns to the ranks, although he may be given other opportunities to advance.

It is interesting to note that the Chilean Pentecostals, especially the larger groups, do not look upon the tent-making ministry as an ideal, although it may well be a necessary step along the road to their ideal, which is that of a full-time pastor fully supported by his congregation. To become a full pastor the candidate has to prove that he has been able to give up his secular occupation because he has gathered a sufficiently large congregation to pay for his material needs. It goes without saying that Pentecostals teach tithing. Outside observers estimate that the average church member does indeed give a minimum of 5% of his income—and this in a country where the annual per capita income is $796 and members come from the poorer classes.

One of the apparent contradictions in the Pentecostal pattern of training is that it feeds into a church structure that while not democratic is totally open. Access to the pastoral office is open to all without exception. In this sense Pentecostalism is a classless hierarchy!

> It is based on a call to the ministry and proof of that calling throughout the stages of a very long process which effects a selection that is looked upon as supernatural. . . . It gives Pentecostalism a healthy dynamic organization, because a community will have no pastor unless it is able to support him, and the candidates for the ministry have to gather a large flock in order to carry out their vocation.[17]

LaLive compared the training process described above as com-

---

17. *Ibid.*

parable to that obtained in the last century by those apprenticed to master craftsmen. A premium is placed upon imitation and collaboration with a strong emphasis upon the pragmatic.

The disciples listen to the master and observe what he does, and then imitate him. The quality of the training therefore depends upon the quality of the master. Obviously, the intellectual training of the Pentecostalist pastor will be neglected in favour of his practical training. He learns how to preach, how to lead the service, how to organize evangelistic campaigns, how to organize the congregation, how to behave as a pastor. . . .[18]

The Pentecostal system of theological education through apprenticeship is found among nearly all popular sectarian movements and was the one usually followed during the first four hundred years of the Christian church. It corrects many (LaLive says all) of the defects found in the traditional Protestant system of ministerial training in the developing countries.

It draws its recruits from the widest possible field; any member of the church can become a pastor, even if he is converted at an advanced age. It gives members a sense of collective responsibility, drawing everyone into evangelism. It stimulates the expansion of the Pentecostalist denominations. And finally it produces pastors who are the genuine expression of the congregations since they do not differ from them either socially or culturally.[19]

Thus, writing in the context of Chile, LaLive concludes his study—

. . . convinced that this system of pastoral training is an important factor in the success of Pentecostalism and that the system of "training by seminary" is not without significance for the problem of the shortage of candidates for the ministry in the Protestant Churches and for their stagnation.[20]

Despite the contribution that Pentecostal patterns of theological education have to make to the total scene, the apprenticeship system for pastoral training has the same weaknesses of any apprenticeship system. Even LaLive admits that ". . . apprenticeship based on observation and imitation emphasizes tradition, which becomes norma-

---

18. *Ibid.*, p. 190.   19. *Ibid.*   20. *Ibid.*, p. 198.

tive and thus tends to reduce the biblical message. . . ."[21] Generally speaking, the learner rises no higher than his model and all too often imitates bad patterns as well as good ones if he has no theoretical base upon which to make corrections.

THEOLOGICAL EDUCATION BY EXTENSION

Theological Education by Extension, or TEE as it is often abbreviated, is simply decentralized theological education. It is a field based approach which does not interrupt the learner's productive relationship to society. Instead of the student coming to the seminary, the seminary goes to the student.

The purpose of decentralization is to extend the resources of theological education to the real leaders of the local congregation, thus enabling them to develop their gifts and ministries so that they can participate more fully and effectively in the full-orbed growth of Christ's church. The extension takes place in several dimensions: geographically to the different areas where students live; culturally in accordance with the customs and needs of each zone; academically to the different levels of secular education; socially to the various classes; ecclesiastically to all present and potential leaders rather than only candidates for ordination; and chronologically to persons of all ages as well as to individuals who desire a program of continuing education through the years. In short, the basic purpose behind the movement is to reach a currently unreached group with ministerial training and to provide a significantly better form of education for those who are reached.

There are three crucial components which make up theological education by extension.

The Weekly Meeting at a Local Center

The first is a meeting, usually weekly, between professor and student at an extension center on a mutually acceptable day and hour. This center is a miniature seminary, although it may be located in a church building, a school, a home, or—as was once the case in Guatemala—under a bridge on the Pan American highway! Ideally,

---

21. *Ibid.*

the center should contain a table and chairs (or other suitable furniture), a blackboard, and a small basic library. The classes last between one and three hours depending on the nature of the subjects and the number of subjects taught. The format of the weekly meeting is that of a seminar. Although a quiz is frequently given at the opening of the session to insure student mastery of cognitive material in the previous week's assignment, the teacher does not lecture. He is thus freed to enable the student to apply biblical training to the life situations which are constantly brought before the class by students already involved in ministry. Peter Savage describes the dynamics of the weekly encounter:

> The meeting does not duplicate any classroom setting. Essentially, it is the place where the tutorial activities between teacher and student are fulfilled. The main learning activity has taken place during the interval between weekly meetings. The main purpose of the meeting is to stimulate the student in his programmed studies by helping him over some conceptual hurdles, while at the same time helping him to come to grips with his material. The professor sees himself as a midwife, helping the student to bring to birth biblical truth in his mind and heart. The student is "in labor." He must go through the birth pangs as he struggles with concepts, ideas, and currents of thought. No longer is he informed of the truth by mere rote memorization. Under the guidance of the Holy Spirit he is helped to come to the light of the truth.[22]

Whereas Savage underscores the importance of struggling with "concepts, ideas, and currents of thought," Paul A. Pomerville points to the affective domain as the critical area of theological education. He is concerned with changed attitudes, values, character, and behavior as well as changed thinking. He sees the learning situation provided by the weekly seminar as highly conducive to the kind of well-rounded learning experience that will help the student be and do as well as know.[23]

---

22. Peter Savage, "A Bold Move for More Realistic Theological Training," *Evangelical Missions Quarterly* V (Winter, 1970), pp. 70-71.

23. Paul A. Pomerville, *Handbook for Theological Education by Extension* (North Sumatra, Indonesia, 1973), p. 41.

Such a weekly encounter held in the setting in which the student lives contributes to a more personal and intimate, indeed, a more vital relationship beween student and professor, than often occurs in formal residential study. Savage comments that through the weekly meeting the professor "rubs shoulders with the students, with their problems, with their pastoral visions and failures."[24] Not only do such encounters involve the professor more deeply in the life of the local churches, but they contribute to a more student-centered, pastorally oriented approach to theological education.

The Self-Study Materials

The second crucial component in decentralized theological education are the self-study materials. These are not miracle books. In fact, at present the majority of extension seminaries are relying upon glorified workbooks keyed either to the Bible or to basic theological texts. A sprinkling of programmed textbooks are also in use. Regardless of the type of self-study materials used, the basic principle remains. The student who actively participates in directed investigation will have a deeper learning experience and retain more than the student who has been spoon fed on lectures in monologue classroom teaching.

Each week at the center, the student is given an assignment based either on his programmed textbook or on his textbook and workbook. During the week he must set aside a total of about five hours per course to work through his assignment, preferably in daily one-hour periods.

It is precisely these self-study materials that make possible the multi-level nature of theological education by extension. Students on all levels, from primary school through university graduates, are enabled to study in the same center. They all study the same subject, but each studies to the depth that his education and intelligence allows him. While one earns a Diploma in Theology the other finishes with a Master of Divinity. Each student covers certain basic core material germane to his subject. The primary school graduate stops

---

24. Savage, *op. cit.*, p. 71.

with the mastery and application of basic content. The high school graduate in addition does more outside reading and is expected to analyze critically what he is taught, as well as apply it. The student with university background is required not only to master, analyze critically, and apply the course content, but is expected to do wide outside reading and write research papers. One of the most exciting classes I ever taught was composed of a telegraph operator with a primary education, an insurance representative with a secondary education, and an engineer with a university degree. The upper and middle-level students served to amplify the perspective of the lower-level student, while the lower-level student forced the middle and upper-level students to express themselves simply and practically.

Not only is learning multi-level, but it is also geared to the situation of the student and to the pace he can maintain. The course load which the student carries is determined by the time he has available. Most persons can handle only one or two courses per year. The above-mentioned telegraph operator handled three, as did a woman accountant in Honduras, who had a long lunch hour in an air-conditioned office. In Guatemala, it was discovered that small shopkeepers with high motivation were able to complete the entire theological curriculum in three years—the same as the residence students! Thus a few students may graduate in three years, some in five, most in seven or eight, a few in twelve or fifteen. Each student advances at his own pace.

Periodic Central Meetings of the Student Body

The third indispensable characteristic of theological education by extension is a periodic regional meeting of the students from various extension centers at a central location. This preserves the sense of community. Savage describes such a gathering:

> Here the leaders from varying strata of society and backgrounds of culture gather to share in a true *koinonia* experience. Voices are blended in a choir; opinions and ideas are merged in plans; experiences and insights are moulded into patterns. The devotional chapel times, the group discussions on relevant church topics, the choir rehearsal, the examinations during the two day

gathering all serve to motivate the student in his programmed studies. He feels he belongs to a wider student community deeply involved in the life of the church.[25]

Although extension education "orthodoxy" calls for monthly meetings, most seminaries find this impractical. Many students work on Saturday, making it impossible to administer examinations to everyone at the same time. Taking key leaders out of their local congregations each month creates ill will toward the program on the part of the pastors and the congregations themselves. Travel costs, which are subsidized, add up. A number of institutions find it far more practical to have quarterly meetings in the form of workshops and retreats in addition to the final gathering of the entire student body for graduation at the end of the school year.

In summary, the three essentials in decentralized theological education are weekly meetings of students and faculty in regional centers, daily study directed through self-study materials, and periodic gatherings of the entire student body for purposes of research, instruction, inspiration, discussion, and recreation. Diagram E clearly sets forth the rhythm of a typical extension program.

Comparison and Contrast

The true genius of theological education by extension, as well as the contribution it can make to theological education as a whole, can perhaps best be seen by comparison and contrast with the other previously mentioned approaches.

Residence. Whereas traditional theological education extracts the student from his environment, decentralized theological education extends the seminary to the student. Traditional theological education seeks to prepare generally inexperienced youth for ministry through intensive academic and incidental practical training. Extension theological education aims to prepare mature persons in ministry through extensive (of longer duration) academic training related to the life

---

25. *Ibid.,* p. 72. However, Savage neglects to mention other important facets of the periodic meeting such as library research and the reception of courses difficult to impart by extension at the present time, i.e., music, literacy, audio-visual education, etc.

Diagram E: The Rhythm of an Extension Program

Annual Convocation

Periodically—one or two days

Weekly Center Meeting

Daily Study

Location	Frequency	Educational Instrument	Library
Home	Daily	Workbook	Personal
Extension Center	Weekly	Professor	Reference
Regional Center	Periodically	Faculty	Research
Headquarters	Annual	Church-at-large	Curriculum

The four locations of action are standard in larger systems. For smaller systems locations "Regional Center" and "Headquarters" may be combined with frequency of meeting being quarterly and including the annual convocation.

Adapted from Ralph D. Winter, "Build the System with Care," *Theological Education by Extension*, p. 429.

which the person lives. It is in-service rather than for-service training. Whereas traditional training concentrates on the education of promising but inexperienced youth, theological education by extension focuses on the education of mature persons with experience in both the church and the world. Thus, it opens the doors of theological education to persons in mid-career and to laymen of all ages desirous of a theological education. It trains both laymen and future clergy together.

Correspondence. Theological education by extension differs from correspondence in that the former allows for systematic personal contact and guidance from the professor while the latter does not. Extension allows no student to study by correspondence. Each professor must have personal contact with every student on a weekly basis. Every student must attend the weekly classes at the local center, which are spent trying to provoke discussion, original thought, and application to the real situation students face. These elements are missing in correspondence courses. Also, extension allows for faster feedback on assignments and examinations than is possible through correspondence study, where innate delayed feedback is often aggravated further by the slowness of the mails so common to the developing nations.

Short-Term Bible Institute. While short-term Bible institutes are keenly aware of the dangers of extracting a person from his environment for long periods of time, their emphasis falls upon intensive doses of residence study for short periods of time. Decentralized theological education is, by contrast, extensive, non-residence, and spread over a long period of time.

Evening Bible Schools. Theological education by extension is similar to the evening Bible schools in that the class often is held in the evening during the free time of the students and the frequency of encounter is weekly rather than daily. However, whereas evening Bible schools tend to limit outside assignments, one of the pillars of theological education by extension is guided daily study aimed at making each student a lifetime learner. Also, generally speaking, rather than the lecture system frequently employed at night Bible schools, extension theological education opts for an inductive educational methodology on the premise that the student remembers best the answers he has worked out for himself.

Apprenticeship. Although theological education by extension incorporates the insights of apprenticeship training in that it recognizes traditional leadership patterns, underscores in-service training, and seeks to train recognized leaders, it also differs drastically from apprenticeship training. The latter is predominantly "non-formal education" by imitation, whereas extension theological education is to date largely formal education complete with required courses, textbooks, assignments, examinations, credits, and diplomas. Nevertheless, theological education by extension has been well received in some Pentecostal circles. Without destroying their apprenticeship system, TEE allows mature pastors and workers to increase their biblical-theological knowledge and improve their ministerial skills without "leaving the streets" and thus destroying their identification with the masses.

Summary. Having scanned the viable options to traditional theological education proposed and employed by various persons and groups, it can be seen that theological education by extension incorporates features from all, yet so blends these insights and characteristics that it constitutes a distinct and timely contribution to the training of the ministry.

> If the extension were just an alternative educational technique it would be worthy of serious interest. But for one curious reason it is far more than that: it allows an entirely new resource to be tapped for formal leadership, it allows the renewal, the building up of the church by means of an entirely new approach. It is not just a different way of hammering Hebrew into students' heads, it is a new way for the living church to deploy its real leadership. The real significance of extension is its ability to do new things in a new age. . . .[26]

---

26. Ralph D. Winter, "An Extension Seminary Manual," *Theological Education by Extension,* p. 390.

Part II

A Brief History of a Young Movement

Chapter IV

FROM LABORATORY TO LAUNCHING PAD

In 1966 theological education by extension (TEE) was limited to a single seminary in one nation. Eight years later the movement encompassed 16,475 students in 182 institutions in 57 countries.[1] Born and nurtured in growing Third World churches, it is now being tried successfully in the United States as well as those in the Third World institutions long dominated by traditional North American and European patterns of theological education. TEE has struck ministerial training with such force that some enthusiasts label it as the most important innovation in theological education in this century. Not only has it responded directly to the felt needs of churches around the world but has had a widespread indirect influence:

> Many institutions and theological educators who do not participate directly in extension programs have, nevertheless, reflected the influence of the movement as they modify their philosophy and methods of teaching. The widespread acceptance of extension studies has also encouraged others to promote other forms of ministerial and lay training which are even less traditional or "non-formal." The whole concept of the ministry has been called into question and is being examined anew from perspectives which are at the same time more pragmatic and more biblical.[2]

Theological education by extension was brought into being in 1963 through an interesting combination of persons and circumstances in an unlikely place—the southwestern corner of Guatemala. During the next four years the innovation spread first to southeastern

---

1. Wayne C. Weld, "The Current Status of Theological Education by Extension," *Theological Education* X, 4 (Summer, 1974), p. 225.
2. *Ibid.*

Guatemala, then to Ecuador, Honduras, the West Indies, Mexico, and Costa Rica. Following a catalytic workshop-consultation held in Armenia, Colombia, in September, 1967, the number of institutions and students involved in extension began to multiply dramatically. The founding of a nationwide interdenominational extension seminary in Colombia during 1969 became the mechanism of advance to South America as institutions in Brazil and Bolivia eagerly adopted the new approach to theological education. By the early 1970's, repercussions began to be felt in the United States as well as in other parts of the world. The dissemination of literature followed by journeys of special teams to Asia and Africa introduced the concept to those continents, where it has also taken root and is beginning to flourish.

The brief history of this young movement—which is just reaching its teen years—has developed in four distinct, though overlapping, stages. They can best be narrated in space-age terminology: from laboratory to launching pad, going into orbit, circling the globe, in-flight corrections.

THE LABORATORY OF EXPERIMENT: GUATEMALA

In 1960, the Presbyterian Church of Guatemala, founded in 1883, numbered 10,000 communicant members with a total community estimated at between 25,000 and 40,000. They lived within a 100 by 300 mile rectangle in the southwestern corner of that nation. Throughout the area was a network of 65 organized congregations, 10 of them in the two major cities of Guatemala and Quezaltenango, plus 140 unorganized preaching points. In this zone, which includes both the steaming costal plains and the Indian highlands, one finds the entire spectrum of Guatemalan society: urban professionals, the rising middle class, rural Latins, both progressive and isolated Indian tribes.

In 1938 the Presbyterians founded a seminary in Guatemala City, the capital, to train leadership for the entire denomination. Attendance ranged from six to twenty students a year during the next quarter-century. Missionary and national professors taught a traditional theological curriculum. The students, largely younger, unmarried men, came mostly from the rural areas, although many also came from the city. The entrance requirement of a complete primary education was laxly enforced. Other students were prepared by the rural presbyteries using a series of books which were studied at home. Examinations were administered by the presbytery every six months. Students were tested on the mastery of the materials studied and then were assigned further work.

However, in spite of the leaders produced through the years via the two channels of seminary and presbytery, many churches remained without pastors, and numerous men trained as pastors were without churches. A 1962 inventory disclosed that after 25 years only ten of the more than 200 students who passed through the seminary were still functioning as pastors. The rest, trained as pastors, were engaged in other occupations.

> The vacant churches were those in climatic zones, locally considered as unhealthy although in rich agricultural zones. The depressed incomes of these areas precluded highly paid ministers from local support. Often students, young and untried, changed their minds about their call to the ministry and never became pastors. Some became disillusioned, expecting from the church what it still was unable to give—full support for a full-time ministry.[3]

In addition to the matter of vacant congregations, another problem reared its head: ". . . how to meet the needs of both city and country churches with their tremendous range of educational, financial and social differences."[4]

Working closely with concerned national leaders, three missionaries—Ralph D. Winter, James Emery, and F. Ross Kinsler—provided the creative input for the now-famous "Guatemala Experiment."

The first step taken was to move the seminary out of the capital city, which was located at one end of the Presbyterian zone, to a rural area in southwestern Guatemala, which is the geographical center of the Presbyterian field of work.

However, even after relocation, it was discovered that the genuine

---

3. James Emery, "The Presbyterian Seminary in Guatemala: Three Years Later 1966," 2. This unpublished dittoed report was later incorporated into the book, *Theological Education by Extension,* where it appears between pages 86 and 101.

4. *Ibid.*

local leaders in the rural area could not even go a few miles to a residence program because of job and family responsibilities.

It was in 1963 that the seminary leaders took the daring step of minimizing their residence program to begin the first extension system. They organized several regional centers where professors could meet for a weekly three-hour period with those who wanted to study. The regional centers were so located that nearly all who desired to study could easily attend. The seminary also paid student travel expenses. In addition, each month during the school year a two-day meeting for all students from all centers was held at the central campus near San Felipe.

To meet the mounting feeling in the urban areas that the cities were being abandoned in favor of a "backwoods" seminary, regional extension centers were also established in Quezaltenango and in the capital city of Guatemala, where a theology department was begun in the new Protestant Mariano Galvez University.

The simultaneous operation of both a residence and an extension program in 1963 placed a severe strain on both personnel and finances. When a study revealed that a full 70 percent of the personnel and 80 percent of the budget were being absorbed in the training of the five residence students while the rest of the resources of the institution served the 65 students in extension, the decision was made to suspend the residence program in order to pour all available resources into the promising extension program.

Another problem soon arose. The take-home studies used by extension students included lengthy reading assignments. These were simply not being digested, especially by the more simple, non-academically oriented rural students. To meet this challenge a series of workbooks based on traditional textbooks but especially geared for personal study were developed over a period of years. This process is still going on and now includes the partial use of programmed instruction.

It seemed that with each solution came another problem. This time it was diversity within the student body. Winter explains that—

> Men of equally keen leadership and spiritual qualification were found within even our own area in two different Indian tribes, and

on three different social levels, as well as with radically different academic backgrounds.[5]

While the very flexibility of decentralized extension centers allowed breathing room for multi-cultural diversity, it was necessary to build a multi-level structure into the texts themselves, thus relating theological studies to the level of secular education previously attained by the student: sixth grade, ninth grade, two years of university. Thus, the Guatemala experiment became not only decentralized and cuturally diverse, but multi-level as well. While all students covered the same basic assignments together, the more advanced students were expected to go a second and third mile in reading assignments and reports, as well as to take on more difficult examinations.

The final basic problem to be solved was that of pre-theological education. Particularly in the rural areas there were many gifted leaders with innate intelligence, but meager academic training. They could not even do the sixth-grade-level courses at the bottom rung. To meet this need for pre-theological education, a second extension program was established on a nationwide, inter-mission basis to help not only prospective seminary candidates but also other interested persons to complete their primary schooling and receive their government recognized diploma.

Not only did the Guatemala experiment prove that it was possible to establish a viable extension system for the education of theological students, but it also produced some unexpected discoveries. Students and faculty who had previously been overlooked suddenly seemed to pop out of the woodwork. The size of the faculty increased to 12 part-time professors in addition to the basic staff of five full-time professors. With no increase in personnel or funds the enrollment increased year by year from 7 to 50 to 88 to 90 to 143 to more than 200 by 1966, before leveling off.

In a typical year an average total of 250 courses are completed (most courses are annual) and at least 150 of the students complete a minimum of one unit. Approximately 10 students graduate per

---

5. Ralph D. Winter, "A Successful Experiment in Taking the Seminary to the Student," *Theological Education by Extension,* p. 127.

year. Most earn a Diploma in Theology, but an increasing number are receiving Th.B. To the surprise of nearly all, many high-caliber, well-educated persons, including university graduates, were attracted. A few Masters degrees have already been earned.

By training men where they lived without uprooting them from their environment, the Seminary was able to reach at least five different subcultures at the same time. Furthermore, although extension study proved more difficult than expected due to the great demand for personal discipline which it laid upon the student, it also proved as a by-product to be a vast screening process. It filtered out unequipped candidates without causing them the shame that had previously resulted when one had to return to his hometown after having dropped out or having been expelled from seminary. Another check showed that rather than closing the door of the ministry to younger men, there were now more younger men than ever before studying, even though the average age of the student was in the thirties. The quality of the academic work also improved over that of the old residence program, due largely to the greater maturity of the students who were in the process of building lifelong personal study habits. In addition, a full theological education was made available to many lay leaders in the congregation who wanted to deepen their faith and understanding without necessarily committing themselves to the pastoral ministry.

The enthusiasm of the faculty in their travels and writings began to arouse the interest of other individuals and groups as well, especially as they saw the clear evidence of the results that were being produced. At first interest was limited largely to Guatemala, although James Hopewell, then director of the Theological Education Fund, learned of the program in late 1963 and visited Guatemala the following year to observe it firsthand. His personal influence as well as his article in the April, 1967, *International Review of Missions,* which spoke favorably of the innovation, undoubtedly influenced others to consider it seriously.[6]

During the last quarter of 1965 the Chiquimula Bible Institute of

---

6. *Ibid.,* p. 309.

the California Friends Mission in Guatemala launched their own program of theological education by extension. They patterned their program after that of their Presbyterian neighbors to the west. One hundred students in 15 centers studied the Old Testament at the diploma level.

In July, 1966, the Committee to Assist Mission Educators Overseas (CAMEO), which stemmed from the liaison between the Inter-denominational Foreign Missions Association (IFMA) and the Evangelical Foreign Mission Association (EFMA), sponsored a seminar for Bible institutes. The gathering was held at the Central American Mission Bible Institute in Guatemala City. Thirty-four delegates from 18 theological training schools located in Middle America and the Caribbean area attended. During this workshop some delegates became acquainted with the Presbyterian experiment and resolved to put it into practice in their own field of work.

＊In October, 1966, the Center of Theological Studies sponsored by the United Evangelical Church of Ecuador, influenced partly by. Hopewell, initiated the first extension program outside of Guatemala. In contrast with previous programs which were denominational in nature, CET enrolled students from three denominations and four independent congregations. Theological education by extension, brought into being and tested in Guatemala, was now clearly moving beyond the laboratory stage.

TOWARD THE LAUNCHING PAD: ARMENIA

Meanwhile, several pioneer programs were initiated during 1967. The Conservative Baptists began a program in the interior of Honduras, which later had to be reconstructed due to the very limited background of the students and incredibly bad roads. The Rev. J. Kenneth Trauger, although not present at the Guatemala seminar, heard of the movement about the same time and after a visit to Guatemala established a center in San Pedro Sula, Honduras, as a pilot project in the Evangelical and Reformed Church. Dr. Samuel Rowen carried the vision to the West Indies, where he not only founded a program, but also published a 57-page pamphlet entitled *The Resident Extension Seminary: A Seminary Program for the Do-*

minican Republic. During the year additional efforts were begun at the Evangelistic Institute of Mexico, and the Methodist Theological Seminary in Costa Rica.

The tiny but growing movement continued to gather momentum. During the January, 1967, meeting of the Latin American Association of Theological Schools—Northern Region (ALET) held at the United Biblical Seminary in Medellín, Colombia, President Plutarco Bonilla of Costa Rica's Latin American Biblical Seminary, wedged two extra hours into the two-day meeting in order to allow Ralph Winter to give an account of the concept of extension theological education in the light of the Presbyterian experience in Guatemala. Winter's presentation fell like a spark into dry tinder due to the frustration with traditional systems of theological education and a growing interest in extension among several of the member schools of the association. ALET proceeded to schedule its next annual workshop on the subject "Extension Education and the Programmed Textbook." It was scheduled to be held in Armenia, Colombia, on the campus of the Christian and Missionary Alliance Bible Institute in September, 1967.

A World Vision Pastor's Conference was also scheduled for Colombia during April, 1967. Winter, now the newly elected executive secretary of ALET, was slated to confront Bible institute leadership with the possibilities of an educational program based upon extension. Prior to the April retreat, Winter, then teaching part-time in the School of World Mission at Fuller Theological Seminary, discovered that four missionaries in the student body were from the area which was to be touched by the Pastor's Conference. Together they drew up a document which reflected their groping toward a viable structure for theological education by extension in the area of Greater Colombia. Winter relates:

> The document was sent to all the institutions of the area, and when the regional subsecretary of ALET, Wallace Rehner, convened a meeting of leaders at the World Vision Pastors Conference in April, it was found that considerable interest already existed. Representatives from twelve different Bible Institutes were on hand and met as a provisional committee agreeing that at the coming ALET workshop on extension there should be an organizing meeting of a "Greater Colombia (Venezuela, Co-

lombia, Ecuador, and Panama) Union of Biblical Institutions" (UNICO).[7]

Although UNICO was not formally established until the Armenia workshop, it was sufficiently functional to act as host for the upcoming workshop.

One major mission agency, the Conservative Baptist Foreign Mission Society, spurred by the importance of these developments, compiled a 23-page sheaf of documents, which was sent out to their missionaries around the globe who were in any way related to the planting of churches or the development of pastoral leadership. They also began to publish an occasional "Bulletin of Extension Seminary Training." Not only did this lay the groundwork for the formation of an association of extension seminaries in Brazil, but it was the first serious attempt to disseminate what was occuring in Central America on a worldwide basis.

The countdown finally reached zero during September 4-9, 1967, when the Armenia workshop finally took place. It not only drew together a number of key persons, but also proved to be the launching pad for the movement from Central into South America.

It was a formal event in the ALET calendar and was subsidized by ALET funds deriving from the Theological Education Fund. It was the constitutional meeting of a new sub-regional association (UNICO) . . . projected an advisory committee for textbook production . . . and proposed an actual curriculum for the joint preparation of the special textbooks so important in extension education . . . named Intertexts. . . . The CLATT office (Latin American Committee on Theological Texts) also . . . derived from this meeting, though not officially, since it is itself an ad hoc structure.[8]

Why was this workshop so decisive to the future trajectory of the extension movement?

---

7. Ralph D. Winter, "The Year of the Breakthrough: 1967," *Theological Education by Extension,* p. 127. The document was also distributed to each of the 400 pastors present at the World Vision Conference for their personal study and reference and to be taken back to their home denominations.

8. Ralph D. Winter, "The Springboard in Colombia," *Theological Education by Extension,* p. 148.

First, it brought together nearly all the persons involved in extension up to that time. The sharing of ideas and experiences stimulated existing programs.

Second, it spurred the founding of new extension programs. At least eight were founded in 1968.

Third, TEE became a known entity. The results of the workshop, the first one wholly dedicated to theological education by extension, were published in a widely distributed booklet entitled *The Extension Seminary and the Programmed Textbook—A Report of a Workshop.* Winter wrote in 1969: "To the date of this writing, there is no other piece of literature that has produced greater serious interest in theological education than the printed report of the workshop . . . in Armenia."[9]

Fourth, the Intertext project, which aimed at the production and distribution of international and interdenominational self-teaching texts or manuals for use as home study materials in extension programs, was established. The various institutions represented at the Armenia workshop formulated a model curriculum. They determined the structure of the books—five modules per lesson, 15 lessons per semester; decided that the intertexts should be geared to the postprimary, or diploma level; agreed that they should be written in Spanish. To implement these decisions two loosely organized structures were set up. One called CATA (Advisory Committee on Self-teaching Texts) and the other CLATT (Latin American Committee on Theological Texts). Although they worked together on the selection of potential authors, the job of the technical advisors who made up CATA was to stimulate and aid authors in the production of materials, while the function of CLATT was ". . . similar to that of a literary agent in working with authors, publishers, contracts, markets, etc. . . ."[10]

---

9. *Ibid.*
10. Ralph R. Covell and C. Peter Wagner, *An Extension Seminary Primer* (South Pasadena, Calif.: William Carey Library), p. 114. The authors devote an entire chapter (pp. 110-117) to the intertext project including the development of CATA and CLATT. Cf. Wayne C. Weld, *The World Directory of Theological Education for Extension,* which clearly explains the relationship among UNICO, CATA, CLATT, ALET, and TEF, pp. 31-32, 102-109, 119-120.

When the delegates came together at Armenia, TEE was still an unknown experiment being carried out by a handful of relatively unknown seminaries. When they concluded their labors a few days later and returned to their respective countries, many were still not fully aware that in those brief days they had "fired the shot heard 'round the world."

From their Armenia launching pad they had engineered the blast-off of TEE.

Chapter V

GOING INTO ORBIT

Having moved beyond its laboratory stage in Guatemala and blasted off from its Armenia launching pad, theological education by extension was streaking into orbit. By 1968, the speed of TEE's acceleration as a movement was attracting continent-wide attention. Interest leaped southward. Visible results were most immediately seen in Bolivia, Colombia, and Brazil.

Interestingly, the extension movement in each of these countries developed along quite different lines: a denominational program in Bolivia; an association of extension theological schools in Brazil; and a vast interdenominational project in Colombia. Each of these new developments awakened widespread interest.

A NEW BASE IN BOLIVIA

Workshops have been a powerful tool in the hand of extension enthusiasts intent upon spreading TEE to new areas. Although recent workshops have stressed the preparation of materials and teaching methodology,

> . . . [the] basic purpose of the earlier workshops on theological education by extension was to introduce the idea and show how this innovation in pastoral training could be relevant to the situation of the delegates to the workshops. The need for national leaders, the biblical concepts of the ministry and other arguments . . . were expressed. Theological educators were made to see the inadequacy of thir own programs and curricula for the preparation of a sufficient number of leaders for the churches. The first workshops depended heavily on the Guatemala model

and promoted the use of materials produced in the Presbyterian Seminary since nothing else was available.[1]

It was Peter Savage and C. Peter Wagner of the Bolivia-based Andes Evangelical Mission who invited Dr. Ralph Winter to hold a workshop in Cochabamba, Bolivia, under the sponsorship of the then functioning Bolivian Association of Theological Schools (ABET).

In response to this workshop, held August 3-7, 1968, 121 delegates representing 27 churches in five countries attended. About half were nationals. Every Bible institute and seminary in Bolivia was represented. Among other things, out of the workshop came the following results:

1. A 37-page report was published containing important guidelines in regard to the theory, form, and content of theological education by extension;

2. The formation of the Andes Association of Theological Education (AADET) was approved;

3. Through the presentations of Peter Savage, programmed instruction was introduced as an integral part of the planning for theological education by extension;[2]

4. It was decided that each denomination was to be left free to develop its own extension program, ". . . especially those which were already operating residential institutions. . . ."[3]

5. A most significant and ambitious extension program was begun in Bolivia through the establishment of the George Allen Theological Seminary of the Evangelical Christian Union (UCE) in 1969. It was this program that provided TEE with a Bolivian base. A national church of about 14,000 members, some 180 churches and 110 pastors, the UCE resulted from the work of several interdenominational missions. Jaime Rios describes the situation facing one sector of this denomination in 1968:

---

1. Wayne C. Weld, *The World Directory of Theological Education by Extension* (South Pasadena, Calif.: William Carey Library, 1973), pp. 131-32.
2. *Ibid.*, p. 141.
3. Ralph R. Covell and C. Peter Wagner, *An Extension Seminary Primer* (South Pasadena, Calif.: William Carey Library), p. 77.

The UCE Churches have been facing a very serious problem in the Cochabamba valley. After making an objective analytical study of sixteen of the twenty five churches of the valley, we found that in the rural areas only two churches have an ordained minister; eight others are pastored by mature, experienced men who nevertheless have had no training whatsoever. Pastors of town or city churches may have had some training, but they are at a great disadvantage in that many of the lay leaders in their congregations have had much more secular education than they. Many such laymen are holding positions of great importance in urban churches without any theological education whatsoever. The problem of giving people a theological education becomes more acute when you take into account the great difference in secular academic background which exists among those who are leaders in the local churches. Of those we had interviewed, some were of the professional level; five had their Bachiller in humanities (high school); eight had their elementary school, and eighteen had only three years of primary.[4]

At that time the only two UCE institutions in the valley were the Quillacollo Bible Institute, which had a residence program for rural Quechua language Indians, and the Emmaus Bible Institute with its residence program for urban Spanish-speaking students. These two institutions, both located in Cochabamba, were merged to form the George Allen Theological Seminary, which embraced urban and rural residential departments and one extension program, each with its own dean, but under one director. The coordination of all phases of ministerial training was placed under the national church. Strategically located extension centers were founded in order to reach those actual leaders who could not come to the seminary. Some succeeded, some failed. "But the number of those who were studying for the ministry rose from the 65 residential students in the two Bible institutes in 1968 to 65 residential plus sixty extension students, making a total of 125 in 1969."[5] The addition of other departments and centers increased the number of extension students to over 150 in 1970 and 231 in 1974.

---

4. James Rios, "Plans for the Future, UCE," *Theological Education by Extension*, p. 195.
5. Covell and Wagner, *op. cit.*, p. 79.

Several of these centers could be reached conveniently only by air. The Rev. C. Peter Wagner told me how Peter Savage, after a Monday morning residence class, flew down to the jungle lowlands for an extension class, hopped back up to Cochabamba for more midweek residence classes, and then flew up to the mountain highlands for an end-of-the-week extension center.

To take into account the academic divergence within the student body, a reality which reflected the diversity within the leadership of the church itself, a five-level study program was set up.

The first is the Certificate level for bilingual students with three years of primary study. The second is the Diploma level for students with six years of primary schooling. The third is the Bachiller "B" for students with three years of secondary education. The fourth is the Bachiller "A" for students with a Bachiller in humanities. The fifth level is the Licenciatura for students who are professional people or who have at least three years of university studies.[6]

Studies on the certificate level, for the student with only three years of primary school, included both ecclesiastical and secular subjects. It was hoped that because of the secular studies taught in the extension program the students would receive a government dispensation freeing them from the necessity of examination over the minor subjects in the government curriculum. In this way they could receive not only a diploma in theology but also their government primary certificate, provided they were able to pass the government examinations which cover the major subjects.

Dr. Winter in December, 1970, described the Bolivian experiment to me as the best model of theological education by extension functioning in Latin America at that time.

However, with the departure of Peter Savage in 1972, the unified structure so ably explained by Wagner and Covell in *The Extension Seminary Primer* divided into separate residence and extension

---

6. James Rios, *op. cit.,* p. 196. The "Bachiller" or "Bachillerato" is a Bachelors Degree, usually earned in the Latin American school system upon completion of full secondary level university preparatory studies. However, many of the subjects studied are usually studied in the United States only in the first year or two of college, i.e., philosophy, sociology, psychology, etc.

programs. It was becoming apparent that the "best working model" wasn't working so well after all.

Savage's initial concern was to advance the total ministerial training in the UCE through the addition of an extension program to the residential programs then functioning. The six areas of need which he felt such a structure could fill included the need for—

> . . . simultaneous training on several different educational levels, teaching more specifically adapted to each subcultural unit, the need for continuing education for pastors of churches experiencing upward social mobility, varying cultural norms for the recognition of maturity and leadership, the problem of semi-literate church leaders incapable of abstract thought and the danger of professionalism in the ministry.[7]

A half-dozen years later, an evaluation made during the Sixth Theological Education Workshop in Cochabamba, January 3-10, 1975, revealed numerous weaknesses (despite the fact that a reported 231 students were involved in extension during 1974, of whom 211 received an average of two courses during the year): failure of students to complete assignments, inadequate programmed materials, lack of teachers trained in the use of programmed learning materials, lack of programmed textbooks prepared by nationals, lack of culturally adapted materials, cross-cultural problems in the areas of communication and understanding between teacher and students, lack of identification of the extension teacher with his students, lack of sufficient theological preparation on the part of the teachers involved, the extended time in order to graduate, and the high subsidy necessary to maintain the program. However, it did appear that in certain rural areas, TEE was serving to strengthen the local church. Furthermore, the challenge of theological education by extension had demonstrated to residence seminaries their need to be more selective in the type of student being admitted, and made them more aware of their need for cultural awareness along with the need to avoid isolating the student from the real world outside.

Thus, while recognizing the immense contribution of TEE, Dr. William J. Kornfield, current president of the George Allen Theologi-

---

7. Covell and Wagner, *op. cit.,* p. 78.

cal Seminary, stresses that the educational challenge facing theological education today is fundamentally cultural in nature and therefore just as applicable to extension as to residence.[8]

A NEW ASSOCIATION IN BRAZIL

The second point on the South American Triangle is Brazil. The leadership crisis in Brazilian Protestantism is especially significant. Not only is Brazil the largest nation in Latin America, with half the population of the entire continent within its borders, but 13 out of every 18 new Protestant Christians in Latin America are Brazilians. With its enormous evangelical base, Brazil contains 72% of all Latin American Protestants. Its 11% annual growth rate brings 500,000 new Protestants into the fold each year, thus producing 4,000 new congregations annually.[9] Yet, despite the mushrooming church expansion, the published figures of the Association of Evangelical Theological Seminaries in Brazil (ASTE) indicate a relatively stationary total of ministerial students.[10]

Few educational innovations have taken root as rapidly as theological education by extension in Brazil. In just seven years TEE has grown from an idea accepted by only a handful of innovators into a movement which has made an impact on approximately one-third of Brazil's theological schools.[11]

Theological education by extension is proving to be a viable means of extending training to church leaders of all ages and educational backgrounds. It reaches these leaders where they live and work; it encourages them to develop their gifts within the context of their present church ministries; it lets them learn at

8. William J. Kornfield, unpublished typescript.
9. Ralph D. Winter, "The New Association in Brazil," *Theological Education by Extension*, p. 203.
10. Richard J. Sturz, "The Crisis in Brazilian Theological Education," *Theological Education by Extension*, p. 204. Cf. Lois McKinney, *TEE Services in Brazil: Purposes, Projects, and Products*, who suggests in a July, 1975, report: "Even though residence seminaries are growing, they are not even beginning to reach the thousands of church leaders who need to be trained."
11. Lois McKinney, *TEE Services in Brazil: Purposes, Projects, and Products*. Pages are not numbered.

their own rate, in their own mode, and in terms of their own goals; it offers them opportunities for life-long continuing education.[12]

What accounts for such rapid growth?

In a sense the soil had already been prepared and the seed sown for the acceptance of theological education in Brazil. A number of leaders had already heard about extension methods being applied elsewhere. Furthermore, the distribution of Conservative Baptist Foreign Missionary Society letters on the theme of extension training indicated that such key theological educators as Dewey Mulholland and Richard Sturz were particularly alert to the potential of the extension movement to aid them in resolving a church leadership crisis. In total isolation, a German Lutheran extension program had sprung into being in the area of Porto Alegre completely apart from the mainstream of the movement. All that was lacking was the germination point of a face to face encounter among theological educators and concerned church leaders. A major workshop scheduled for August, 1968, and organized by former students of Fuller School of World Mission who had returned to the field filled that lack.

Growing directly out of the August workshop attended by 65 persons from 23 theological training institutions, the Evangelical Theological Association for Extension Training (AETTE) was formally constituted on October 12, of the same year, with 43 delegates from 27 institutions in attendance. Administered by a six-man board of directors responsible to the annual General Assembly, the purposes of the association include the provision of methodological orientation for extension teaching, the preparation of materials conducive to this type of teaching, the circulation of information useful to the members as well as the promotion of consultations, workshops, and other gatherings to further the extension movement in Brazil. Present services also include the publication of a quarterly bulletin and catalogs of auto-didactic materials.

At an April, 1969, workshop the textbook-producing arm of

---

12. *Ibid.*

AETTE was set in motion with the 1970 school year set as target for the production of the first texts.

Richard J. Sturz classifies the April meeting as "highly productive." With the invaluable help of Peter Savage from Bolivia the measurable objectives for the curriculum were set up and AETTE was drawn into closer cooperation with the advisory committee for authors writing self-instruction texts for UNICO. A curriculum was drawn up for those with only primary education. The specific objectives for the individual courses of the first two years were worked out, and the authors were chosen for them. A series of workshops was held in 1969 and 1971 to facilitate the planning and writing of texts. Twenty were already in use by the beginning of 1972, and by mid-1975 a total of almost 50 auto-didactic texts have been prepared by member schools.

The theological education by extension movement in Brazil has continued to grow, somewhat in isolation from the movement in Spanish-speaking Latin America. About 4,500 students are enrolled in 36 institutions, most of them in the São Paulo area. In production of programmed materials Brazil has now advanced considerably beyond its Spanish-speaking counterpart. Much of this success is due to the work of Dr. Lois McKinney, CAMEO's field consultant, who also serves as executive secretary of AETTE and as coordinator of graduate studies at São Paulo's Baptist Theological faculty. She reports that since her arrival in Brazil, in February of 1974, . . .

> The CAMEO Internships in Curriculum Development Program has taken root. Eleven theological institutions are sponsoring training programs; twenty-one Brazilian interns are preparing themselves to be writers and educators for theological education by extension (TEE). . . . Several theological schools have begun using the internship study guides to train their teachers and improve their programs. . . . At least three seminaries are beginning master's programs with emphasis in theological education. . . . Some publishers of theological texts, Sunday school materials and leadership training courses are considering the possibilities of programmed instruction. . . . More leaders are becoming aware of the theoretical implications of TEE (as part of a trend toward non-formal education). . . .[13]

13. *Ibid.* Cf. Wayne C. Weld, "The Current Status of Theological Education

Current efforts of the TEE movement in Brazil are aimed at encouraging wider acceptance, improved quality, and rapid nationalization. "If present trends continue, writes McKinney, Brazil may well become the first nation in the world where extension (and other nonformal) modes of theological education are generally accepted, high in quality, and thoroughly nationalized!"[14]

A NEW SEMINARY IN COLOMBIA

The third point of the South American Triangle which Winter affirms "offers so much hope for the extension movement in Latin America today and tomorrow" is Colombia.[15]

Whereas extension programs organized before the Armenia Workshop had been largely limited to single denominations working in a relatively small geographical area, the unique development in Colombia was the formation of a national interdenominational seminary which elicited the cooperation of more than a dozen denominations and missions under one board of directors, with a single executive committee and president. In November, 1968, the United Biblical Seminary of Colombia, with 24 years of service as a denominational and interdenominational seminary, extended its ministry by reorganizing in four divisions: a continuing residence division in Medellín, the nation's industrial capital, and three extension divisions—one in the Medellín vicinity, another in the largely rural zone surrounding Cali, and a third in the urban area of Bogotá. Each of the extension divisions, which in turn was composed of various centers, had its own dean, registrar, and treasurer.

In 1971, the seminary added a fifth division, which is closely related to the predominantly rural Caribbean Bible Center in Sincelejo, then operated by the Latin American Mission. In reality this has been considered a denominational program which receives support and orientation from the United Biblical Seminary, although the

by Extension," *Theological Education* X, 4 (Summer, 1974), p. 230. Cf. F. Ross Kinsler, "Revisita a Sud America—Junio 16 a Julio 14 de 1974," *ALISTE* II, i (Julio de 1974), pp. 1-4.

14. *Ibid.*
15. Ralph D. Winter, "The Nationwide Seminary in Colombia," *Theological Education by Extension*, p. 209.

seminary does not give credit for the many courses taught at the certificate level.

Thus, the United Biblical Seminary became in reality a nationwide network of decentralized cells carrying on theological education in cooperation with a traditional residence program. All of them followed a single curriculum, studied the same textbooks, achieved to the same academic norms, and charged the same uniform fee for matriculation and tuition.

By 1971 there were 25 centers, eight full-time and 22 part-time professors, and 156 students, 130 of whom were studying at the diploma level while the remaining 26 study at the bachiller level. By 1973, a total of 224 students had been enrolled.

Groups which cooperated in the founding of the United Biblical Seminary included the Christian and Missionary Alliance, Evangelical Covenant, General Conference Mennonites, Oriental Missionary Society, Latin America Mission, Mennonite Brethren, and Overseas Crusades. The Gospel Missionary Union and Wesleyan Mission cooperated on an unofficial basis. Additional evangelical groups saw the value of this new development and cooperated in those geographical areas where they had established congregations.

Winter attributed the reality of the new interdenominational seminary not only to ". . . the diplomacy and good will of the Oriental Missionary Society . . . ," but also to the "fact that the evangelical church in Colombia has been a relatively small, persecution-battered movement. . . ."[16] This may help to explain the sense of community and mutual confidence which initially made possible this new type of seminary.

Unfortunately, the initial enthusiasm that sparked the united effort has somewhat waned. The various cooperative groups have tended to drift once again toward denominational isolation. In a personal letter dated February 27, 1975, Wayne C. Weld, until recently rector of the United Seminary and now professor of missions at North Park Seminary, Chicago, indicated that the general board of the seminary was dissolved in early 1975. He added, "The divisions continue to

---

16. *Ibid.*

function . . . and all of them have the right to use the name 'Seminario Bíblico Unido,' but there is no longer any body which meets periodically to coordinate activities of the divisions." The coordination for the publication of materials and the evaluation and revision of curriculum has been assumed by UNICO.

As in Bolivia, the existence of both a residence and an extension division with the structure of the same institution threw needed light on the potential opportunities and conflicts which may develop in such a situation. While Weld concedes that ". . . there are various advantages in having the extension program tied to a residence program— visibility accreditation, maintenance of levels of study, a body of theological educators to prepare materials and aid in teaching and administration, . . ." he also warns that ". . . there can also be a tug of war between the two programs."[17]

Despite the fact that the unified structure is in serious trouble at present, theological education by extension has definitely taken root in Colombia. Weld reports that as of September, 1973, a total of 1,483 students were enrolled in 100 centers operated by ten institutions which represented some fifteen missions or denominations.[18] The number continues to increase.

Out of his experience with TEE as it found expression in the United Biblical Seminary, Weld makes ten suggestions.[19] Although having to do specifically with the program of the United Biblical Seminary, they also have a great deal of general pertinence for extension programs.

1. The denominations must be sold on theological education by extension as at least one of the official pastoral and lay training programs of the denomination. If extension is regarded as a second-rate program which is sufficient for laymen but which could never lead to

---

17. Weld, *The World Directory of Theological Education by Extension*, p. 55.
18. Weld, "The Current Status of Theological Education by Extension," *Theological Education* X, 4 (Summer, 1974), p. 230.
19. Weld, *The World Dictionary of Theological Education by Extension*, pp. 64-66. Although abbreviated, the suggestions are taken directly from Weld, often using his exact words.

ordination, the potential leaders of congregations are not going to waste their time with it.

2. More students can be reached if they are taught within the program of their own congregations. Not only does the organization of centers in local congregations insure that studies are related to local problems and opportunities, but it also relates extension training to the work of the denomination in general.

3. A drop-out rate of up to 50% is acceptable as long as the right people are being attracted to and maintained in extension studies.

4. TEE should be utilized as an instrument for the continuing education of pastors. Ideally, through such a program pastors should be encouraged and guided to become teachers of the extension studies in their own congregations.

5. Nationals must assume greater responsibility not only for teaching, but also for the administration and promotion of extension programs. Competent nationals are also needed to write new extension materials and to revise present materials in order to adapt them better to local needs.

6. Workshops for extension teachers stressing group dynamics, demonstration classes, and supervised experience are essential.

7. At least once a semester if not more frequently there should be a meeting which provides for wider fellowship, corporate worship, and special studies.

8. Intermediate goals should be set up to encourage students who see the completion of studies as a very distant goal.

9. Greater flexibility in the curriculum is necessary so that students can develop their gifts for teaching, preaching, personal evangelism, administration, or any other ministry.

10. More attention should be given to low-level studies, where most of our church people find themselves.

When theological education by extension first went into orbit, the initial successes of the new base in Bolivia, new association in Brazil, and new seminary in Colombia created a wave of euphoria that left the impression with many people that extension was a panacea capable of resolving the inherited problems of imported traditional patterns and making up the deficiencies of previously employed alternative forms of theological education.

It was during this same period of euphoria that TEE began to circle the globe. While it is beyond the scope of this book to chronicle this development, it is important to note briefly how it spread beyond Latin America to other Third World churches as well as to mention its potential for the United States.

Chapter VI

CIRCLING THE GLOBE

Most of the previously mentioned workshops in Latin America which introduced the concept of decentralized theological education were underwritten by the Theological Education Fund of the World Council of Churches.

BEYOND LATIN AMERICA

However, the first workshop drawing people from all over the world was the work of a new force on the scene. The active and resourceful coordinator of the Committee to Assist Missionary Education Overseas (CAMEO), Dr. Raymond B. Buker, Sr., was quick to recognize the potential of the extension seminary. He organized a seminar on extension education following the annual meeting of the National Association of Evangelicals (NAE) in Philadelphia in April, 1968. There the groundwork was laid for a workshop on theological education by extension held in Wheaton, Illinois, during December of that year. One hundred twenty-one persons representing 30 missions attended.[1]

> CAMEO has not excluded from its meetings representatives from agencies not members of either EFMA or IFMA, anymore than the Theological Fund has excluded institutions unrelated to the World Council. . . . However, it is fair to say that the vast majority of those attending the Seminary Extension Workshop at Wheaton were related to the former.[2]

Hundreds of copies of the 120-page report of the Wheaton workshop

1. Ralph D. Winter, "A Revolution Goes into Orbit," *World Vision Magazine* XIV (November, 1970), p. 14.
2. *Ibid.*, p. 16. Cf. Wayne C. Weld, *The World Directory of Theological Education by Extension*, pp. 35-38.

were distributed around the world. Although extension programs continued to multiply in Latin America, there was no immediate response from Asia and Africa. "Men representing missions in Africa and Asia carried the ideas home with them, but it needed some time to germinate and bear fruit."[3]

Meanwhile, decisions made by the Theological Education Fund continued to fan the flame of the extension movement. "Their interest not only helped in the pilot stage of the Guatemalan program but made possible a bulletin, *The Extension Seminary*, which is available in both English and Spanish, and goes into 1,000 schools around the world." Then, in early 1970, the TEF sent out 404 copies of the huge 648-page anthology, *Theological Education by Extension*, to key schools around the world. Edited by Ralph Winter, the collection of documents contains reports of workshops crucial in the development of the extension movement, including the one at Wheaton; lectures and articles selected from sometimes obscure sources; and a practical manual for the development and implementation of an extension seminary. Response was immediate.

> Individual mission agencies bought copies of the above books for their educators: United Presbyterians sent out 40. Christian and Missionary Alliance 100, United Methodists 160, Assemblies of God 200.[4]

An expanding literature increased the receptivity to the concept of theological education by extension to the point that CAMEO laid plans for eight workshops on extension to be held in Africa and Asia during August and September of 1970.

Ted Ward of Michigan State University and Samuel Rowen of West Indies Mission were the team that traveled to Ethiopia, Kenya, Nigeria, and Rhodesia. Ward's book, *Programmed Instruction for Theological Education by Extension*, provided another tool for the growing movement.

The Asian team consisted of C. Peter Wagner of the Andes Evan-

---

3. Wayne C. Weld, *The World Directory of Theological Education by Extension*, p. 37.

4. Ralph D. Winter, "The Acorn That Exploded," *World Vision Magazine* XIV (October, 1970), p. 18.

gelical Mission and Ralph Covell of the Conservative Baptist Seminary in Denver, Colorado. They traveled to Taiwan, Indonesia, Vietnam, India, and Singapore. Their four-day workshops drew over 300 nationals and missionaries. Not only did workshops impart the concepts and methodology of theological education by extension, but also led on many occasions to the formation of regional or national continuing committees which in turn have co-ordinated further workshops, the production of materials, and have been the basis for the formation of associations of institutions working in extension.

The June, 1970, issue of the *Theological Education Newsletter*, published by the National Council of Churches, reported:

> News comes in sporadically from other parts of the world about new extension programs and proposals. Apparently there are at least two extension ministerial training programs operating in England. There is an Extension Education Committee working out plans for Indonesia. Extension workshops have already been held in the Philippines, and further workshops are being contemplated for Taiwan, Hong Kong, Thailand, and Viet Nam. Proposals for extension theological training are taking shape in Ethiopia, Sierra Leone, and Tanzania.[5]

By mid-1974, TEE had spread to thirteen countries in Africa and twelve in Asia. A total of 2,240 students were enrolled in 63 institutions.[6] Permanent regional and national extension committees as well as some associations of extension institutions are now functioning in numerous countries. Recent visits to Asia by F. Ross Kinsler and to Africa by James Emery report increasing interest and growth of the movement in those areas. Recent books by D. Leslie Hill, *Designing a Theological Education by Extension Program: A Philippine Case Study,* and Paul A. Pomerville, *Theological Education by Extension,* published in Indonesia, are further evidence of the growing maturity of the extension movement in Asia.

Weld summarizes the global influence of the movement:

> Today it is a worldwide movement which has gained recognition from missionaries and nationals, from educators and evangelists,

5. *Ibid.*
6. Wayne C. Weld, "The Current Status of Theological Education by Extension," *Theological Education* X, 4 (Summer, 1974), p. 226.

from executives and local pastors and laymen. Associations of theological schools find they must take a position with regard to the movement. Denominations are forming policies and in a few cases denominational programs for extension. Periodicals at home and abroad cannot afford to ignore this movement which has offered so much hope for resolving, at least in part, the urgent matter of pastoral training. . . . It is apparent that theological education by extension is here to stay as one of the most important new movements within the Church in our age.[7]

POSSIBILITIES IN THE UNITED STATES

Theological educators in the United States have not overlooked the possibilities for extending the ministry of seminaries. In recent years many institutions have begun programs of continuing education for the clergy. These programs usually require that the student attend classes at least one day a week at the seminary. For convenience, classes are often grouped in three-hour blocks. Outside reading is done and assignments are completed at home or in the seminary library if time and distance permit.

Almost inevitably, however, the student must travel to the centrally located seminary. When professors do journey out to decentralized locations in regional zones, the courses are generally of a shorter duration and do not carry academic credit. Pittsburgh Theological Seminary, for instance, has offered continuing education courses for ministers in regional centers for years, but on a noncredit basis.

A more daring experiment has been undertaken by Bloy House, an Episcopal seminary in California, which trains mid-career persons for the Episcopal priesthood on weekends in a residence setting. San Francisco Theological Seminary established a program leading to the S.T.D. which requires the candidate to spend three summers in residence in alternate years. Between residence periods his reading is guided and his project work is supervised according to agreed-upon programs tailor-made during his residence study. Thus while San Francisco Seminary does offer credit for parish-based parish-oriented studies, it does not provide for the regular weekly contact of an

---

7. Weld, *The World Directory of Theological Education by Extension*, p. 39.

extension system. New York Seminary now offers urban-oriented non-residence theological studies. Lancaster Theological Seminary has launched a program to train undergraduate students through an entirely field-based middle year. Field education programs have taken on a new seriousness in U.S. seminaries and field-oriented professional doctoral programs are becoming the rule rather than the exception. Internships and Clinical Pastoral Training experiences have proliferated as have continuing education programs. Many seminaries now offer a two-year Masters degree in religious study to equip the lay person who seeks to prepare himself to serve Christ more capably in a vocation other than the professional pastorate. Fuller Theological Seminary apparently became the first United States seminary actually to begin a fully accredited undergraduate extension system when it opened a regional center in Fresno, California, in the fall of 1971.[8] By the fall of 1973, it had added centers in Seattle, Bakersfield, and Los Angeles with a total enrollment of 110. The largest extension seminary in the United States, the American Baptist Theological Seminary of Nashville, Tennessee, reported a January, 1973 enrollment of 693 students in 37 centers. And by 1974 at least one Canadian institution had a large extension program in operation.

An important paper prepared by F. Ross Kinsler, professor of New Testament at the Evangelical Presbyterian Seminary of Guatemala, while on furlough at Pittsburgh Theological Seminary during 1969, made a plea to "extend the seminaries" and listed six concrete ways in which this can be done.[9] His suggestions remain pertinent although some have since been implemented.

He begins with an analysis of current trends which he himself admits may appear disjointed and pessimistic: a cry for relevance, movement toward a free curriculum, increasing replacement of lectures by seminars, financial crisis, the gulf between clergy and laity. However, Kinsler suggests that these difficuties, seen from a different

___

8. Anonymous, "Recent Growth of the Extension Movement," *Theological Education Newsletter* (June, 1970), p. 1.

9. F. Ross Kinsler, "Extend the Seminaries!" *Theological Education by Extension,* pp. 248-255. This writer was privileged to read the manuscript in its pre-publication form. Cf. Ralph D. Winter, "The Possibilities in the United States," *Theological Education by Extension,* pp. 240-245.

vantage point, may present possibilities, not for the seminary to curtail her contribution to the life and mission of the church, but rather to expand it. The vantage point he suggests is that of decentralization or extension.

> The seminary would continue to be the primary institution of theological education, defining objectives, setting academic standards, appointing faculty, and providing basic curricular materials. Accreditation for degrees would be based entirely on comprehensive examinations and papers, and bibliographical guides would set out clearly the areas of basic knowledge and competence necessary to pass these requirements. More specific course outlines, programmed texts, and other material could be prepared.[10]

Thus, although the residence seminary would continue to be the primary institution of theological education, the program itself would operate through a network of regional centers with classes held weekly or bi-weekly and the actual time schedule tailored to fit the needs of the students. These periodic meetings would assume the form of seminars "centering on understanding and application rather than information; the latter would be left to guided reading and programmed materials."[11]

The staff could be made up not only of professors from the central institutions, but professors from other institutions, as well as gifted pastors and laymen from the churches, all depending upon the circumstances. While course offerings would probably be rather limited and vary in each center yearly due to the necessity of following a teaching cycle for best deployment of faculty, students would be free to take any number of courses depending upon such factors as established prerequisites, available staff and materials, and their own time and ability. They would apply for the comprehensive examination according to measured achievement.[12]

Kinsler is quick to point out the advantages of such a program: nurture is left to the local congregations; studies are relevant because they are carried out in the context of the world; the program could be self-supporting and thus capable of infinite expansion. Kinsler concludes his argument:

---

10. *Ibid.,* pp. 247-248.   11. *Ibid.,* p. 248.   12. *Ibid.*

A decentralized seminary would . . . be ideally suited for the theological education of ministers because it would adjust its program to their schedule and needs without taking them away from the world and the church and their means of support. This structure would allow for a more natural development of leadership in the church and perhaps go a long way toward bridging the gap between clergy and layman. Throughout the paper the implied objective of decentralization is to mobilize the church in mission.[13]

Kinsler explains various possible programs in the order in which the typical seminary could most easily extend its existing program.

First, he mentions the continuing education of practicing ministers. Instead of the common single dose at a summer institute of theology, he suggests spreading out continuing education so as to intersperse personal study with classroom teaching, thus providing an opportunity for application of learning within the framework of corrective means. A person may proceed at his own rate, taking from two to six years to earn an advanced professional degree. He suggests that seminaries begin modestly with a center or two, about 50 miles away from the center campus. Kinsler believes that opportunities for such a program are boundless.[14]

Second, Kinsler lists seminary internships. He notes that the first difficulty of existing internship programs is lack of effective supervision. The second is that they add to the number of years required to attain the basic M.Div. degree. However, believing that regional centers can serve more than one purpose, Kinsler outlines another possibility:

If the seminary interns were related to regional centers, they could both receive supervision and earn academic credits by attending weekly seminars and carrying on a full study program. Both their theological studies and the internship experience would be heightened and they would not be held back in reaching the M.Div. It is conceivable that many of the courses at the regional center would be the same ones offered for pastors in the continuing education program and the weekly seminars would be

13. *Ibid.*, p. 249.
14. *Ibid.*, p. 250.

enriched through this egalitarian participation of seminarians and pastors.[15]

Kinsler even goes on to raise the possibility of cutting the on-campus M.Div. program to two years if the majority of seminary students were to opt for the above-mentioned possibility. Some seminaries have now instituted such a program.

Third, Kinsler focuses on theological education for laymen. Regional centers with classes adapted to student schedules place the seminary within reach of the layman. Kinsler feels the most effective way to proceed is ". . . to set up seminars with stiff reading requirements and academic credit and thus select relatively small groups of serious minded men . . ." some of which may be open to ministers and interns also, thus providing not only a healthy dialogue for participants, but making double use of the professor's time as well.[16] Kinsler envisions several purposes being fulfilled via this route, the most prominent being an awakening of the realization that God has given the ministry to the whole church rather than a selected class of professionals. One Presbyterian church in Michigan has transformed its adult Sunday school into a full-fledged extension seminary using a great deal of the curriculum and materials developed by the Presbyterian Seminary in Guatemala. Nearly 50 ardent Christian laymen participate. Many are medical doctors and university professors. The church is even exploring the possibility of securing academic recognition for the courses through the Guatemala seminary.

Other purposes capable of realization through such a program include the surfacing of experienced, world-oriented leadership for the life of the local congregation and, in the case of laymen, the pursuit of his vocation with theological insight. On a more pragmatic fashion, but with overtones of eloquence, he advocates:

> Rather than close rural parishes for purely economic reasons . . .
> let the layman fill those vacancies. Rather than encourage the
> worker-priest idea for the industrial mission and other specialized
> ministries, let the laymen become priests to their own kind. Rather
> than give token participation to laymen in the worship of the

---

15. *Ibid.,* p. 251.
16. *Ibid.*

church one Sunday out of the year, give them full participation throughout the year. Rather than move toward increasingly larger church staffs and multiple professional staffs, encourage the existence of smaller churches or at least encourage the laymen in larger ones to form and lead small groups of meaningful size which are related to their professions, residential communities, and interests. Rather than limit the church's participation in the social revolution to a rather small circle of radical clergymen, who often scandalize rather than lead the church, let the laymen, who have in their hands the means of shaping business and government and community life, enter into and influence the social revolution constructively.[17]

A fourth possibility suggested by Kinsler is the full preparation for ordination of laymen, especially for mid-career or post-career candidates. Persons whose vocations have been awakened late in life could be trained through an extension system, thus bringing to bear upon their theological subjects their wealth of experience as well as permitting them to be trained without subsidy from the seminary or salary loss for family support. Closely related would be the opportunity to test one's vocation before burning one's bridges. With early retirement becoming more and more common, the possibility of a second career in the pastoral ministry becomes quite feasible.

A small or large number of laymen could be encouraged to enter theological training, beginning at any point in their first career, adding new dimensions of service to their lives and new gifts of ministry to the church and to the world.[18]

Fifth, Kinsler suggests that theological education by extension offers genuine possibilities for the university scene. He states that perhaps ". . . the structure and discipline of an academic program, sponsored by a seminary or a group of seminarians would fill the need for a serious presentation of the Christian faith, dialogue with other disciplines, and theology training for both students and faculty."[19] The program could operate with its weekly seminars on or near the campus with courses—whether geared to the university or basic seminary

17. *Ibid.*, p. 252.
18. *Ibid.*, p. 253.
19. *Ibid.*

courses—reflecting the interests and ferment of the campus situation. Academic credit could be given either by a seminary toward a M.A.R. or by some department within the university. As the tendency for seminaries to cluster around major universities or complexes of universities increases, the possibilities for finding personnel for this kind of program should also increase. Kinsler concludes, "Theological study should not be limited to post-graduate ministerial candidates as it has largely been in the past."[20]

Finally, Kinsler views the theological education by extension as a key to the training of minority group leadership.

> One analysis of the problem goes like this—taking the negro minority as an example. The proportion of negroes who go to college is relatively small; only very few of those who graduate consider going to seminary; and among those who do obtain a theological degree even fewer are really prepared for service in black communities or are really willing to serve where the need is greatest. On the other hand these same communities, particularly the churches, have produced outstanding natural leadership, and these men are quite capable of serious theological study within the context of their family-work-church responsibilities. We have mentioned previously the need for the selection and natural development of leadership in the churches. This principle is particularly important in minority group churches.[21]

Kinsler recognizes the possible problems in changing entrance requirements and even the granting of different level diplomas and degrees which such an approach poses. Nevertheless, he feels that the approach would reach more persons who are the real leaders of their communities. Also, he feels that the total investment is significantly smaller than the cost of extracting the same people out of their communities to be sent through college and seminary and then returned again to their communities.

The underlying question beneath all of his proposals, contends Kinsler, is the purpose of the seminaries. He holds that seminaries exist in order to help the churches carry out their mission in the world. With that as his touchstone, he challenges the seminaries to

---

20. *Ibid.*
21. *Ibid.*, pp. 253-254.

ask how their present structure and programs measure up. Kinsler is hopeful

> . . . that the seminaries, which are now going through unprecedented changes in this country, will discover new, flexible, dynamic ways to extend their role and greatly further the church's mission in the world.[22]

---

22. *Ibid.*, p. 254.

Chapter VII

IN-FLIGHT CORRECTIONS

By the early 1970's, it was becoming increasingly apparent that certain aspects of theological education by extension were in need of in-flight corrections.

TEE was being exported from Latin America by euphoric enthusiasts as a panacea for the ills of Third World theological education precisely at the moment when serious questions were being raised about its value and hastily erected extension structures in Colombia and Bolivia were showing signs of cracking, if not crumbling altogether.

In late 1971, James Goff, a former Presbyterian missionary to Colombia and a bitter opponent of church growth theory as well as theological education by extension unleashed a highly polemic article in the World Council of Churches' sponsored *Risk* magazine.

Despite its wild inaccuracies, Goff did succeed in pinpointing three areas which have been of concern not only to opponents of theological education by extension, but to its more astute advocates as well.

IDEOLOGICAL

The first is ideological. It centers on the content of what is taught in extension seminaries. Goff charged that TEE is a perfect tool of indoctrination for right-wing forces aimed at reproducing carbon copies of their mentality on a grand scale. He alleged that in general the missionaries who support the movement:

> ... have mentalities which are firmly committed to the Cold war Mythology of communism versus the free world. They abhor socialism and give allegiance to the free enterprise system. They are

112

conservative in their political, social, economic and theological point of view. They are anti-ecumenical, anti-Roman Catholic, anti-World Council and anti-National Council of Churches. They are committed to developmentalism in Latin America. They have a horror of revolution and they advocate a respect for the powers that be by sacralizing the structures of a society. . . .[1]

Goff claimed that these attitudes and values carried over into the teaching and textbook preparation in a calculated way in order to manipulate the thousands of Latin American pastors and leaders who study by extension. In reply to Goff's first accusation, F. Ross Kinsler, a thoroughgoing evangelical, noted in a letter to Goff that the *Risk* article had only served to polarize the extension movement by identifying it *per se* with extreme right-wing thought. While agreeing that it has generally been the conservative evangelical groups which have taken the initiative in the use and spread of the extension concept, he maintained that TEE is not intrinsically or essentially linked with any particular school of thought.

If the conservatives give it their own ideological definition, that was only to be expected. If others had made use of it—as they are now beginning to do—they would have given it their own connotations. As Freire says, no educational program is ideologically neutral.[2]

Kinsler went on to underscore the need to make a clear distinction between the extension concept and the particular political orientation of those who use it.

METHODOLOGICAL

Goff's second area of concern is methodological. One of the essential elements in extension methodology is the use of self-study materials. The use of workbooks and the later emphasis upon introduction of programmed instruction is the natural result of the search for more adequate ways to guide students in their home study.

Ted and Margaret Ward made clear the difference that exists

---

1. James Goff, "Exalt the Humble," *Risk* VII, 2 (1971), pp. 30-36. Due to working with a Xerox copy of the article, it has been impossible to determine the exact page of the quotation.
2. Personal letter of F. Ross Kinsler to James Goff, March 13, 1972.

between programmed instruction and workbooks. The distinction is important because workbooks have sometimes been wrongly referred to as semi-programmed materials.

> Workbook-style materials are primarily useful in developing the skill of locating information. In contrast programmed instruction is more useful for establishing the use of information. . . . The idea of a workbook is essentially that of a book to direct work. The idea of programmed instruction is essentially that of a book to direct learning. . . . Programmed instruction is not merely an alternate form of "homework," it is an alternate form of teaching.[3]

Programmed instruction, then, seeks to guide the student systematically and progressively toward the attainment of his objectives without the need of a teacher or other aids. It contains three essential elements.

First, the course content is ordered in a logical and progressive manner so as to facilitate the learning process by moving from the known to the unknown, from the simple to the complex.

Second, the student demonstrates his comprehension of his new knowledge by applying it immediately as part of a step-by-step process which may involve answering questions, doing exercises, or solving problems.

Third, the material itself permits the student to check his use of the new knowledge point by point so as to reinforce what has been learned, thus insuring his progress and leading him by steps to more complex and advanced materials.

The smallest units in programmed instruction, called frames, usually contain four elements: information, a question or assignment, space for the students' response, and lastly the correct answer. The above format is just a part of programming, because, in order to be an effective teacher, the programmed instruction must be based on rigorous analysis of the final desired objectives: the capacity of the student and the specific steps that will guide him successfully to the attainment of those objectives.

---

3. Ted and Margaret Ward, *Programmed Instruction for Theological Education by Extension* (East Lansing, Mich.: Committee to Assist Missionary Education Overseas, 1970).

Goff identifies this tendency toward a workbook methodology and programmed instruction as thought control, aimed at producing domesticated persons unable to think for themselves. He charges:

Theological education in this system is not a freedom spawning, unpredictable, liberating encounter. It is information which can be programmed and fed to the pupil in pill size doses . . . and the technique of programmed learning makes spoon fed indoctrination possible. There is a right answer to every question because most of the questions are trivial.[4]

While Goff has undoubtedly overstated his case, there has been a tendency on the part of some extension leaders to over-identify TEE with the use of programmed instruction as if they were inseparable. For instance, C. Peter Wagner wrote in 1971: "By now it has become clear that programmed materials are even more than a cog in the wheel of the extension seminary—they are really the bearings that keep the whole machine running smoothly."[5]

Emery provides a more balanced perspective. In a 1971 letter to Goff, he pointed out that the use of workbooks and programmed instruction attempts to provide the student who has little experience in reading as well as limited access to information with an inductive study methodology.[6] Inductive study is essentially an effort to provide the student with tools by which he can come to understand what an author says and then, upon relating his ideas with other information and with life itself, evaluate what he says. Bible study requires this capacity and the same serves equally well to master any other discipline. Emery argues that inductive study and programmed instruction are perfectly compatible providing that the object of the programmed material is to teach the student to think for himself. By the time the student finishes the course of study, he has the skills and incentive to continue reading. Emery adds that in his experience most

---

4. Goff, *op. cit.*
5. Ralph R. Covell and C. Peter Wagner, *An Extension Seminary Primer* (South Pasadena, Calif.: William Carey Library, 1971), p. 110. For a strong reaction to this point of view from within the evangelical tradition cf. Edwin Brainerd, "The Myth of Programmed Texts," *Evangelical Missions Quarterly* X, 3 (July, 1974), pp. 219-23.
6. Personal letter of James Emery to James Goff, December 29, 1971.

do continue to read and that they choose their own books.

Thus, rather than limiting the student, programmed instruction as employed by theological education by extension frees the student to continue his education by equipping him not only with the basic knowledge ncessary, but also with the capacity to read and reflect for himself. In fact, a course on pastoral theology developed and taught at Mexico's United Evangelical Center employs a workbook that often disagrees with the standard textbook employed and constantly challenges the student to draw his own conclusions based upon his own understanding of both the Bible and his culture.

Furthermore, the weekly seminars are built largely on a foundation of discussion which poses problems and tries to relate the information which the student has gained to their solution.[7] One recent book on TEE even goes so far as to state: *"Never, never, never is the extension leader to lecture!"*[8] The use of programmed instruction or workbooks frees the class time precisely for the kind of dialogue that stimulates creative thinking. Time is not lost by repetition of basic information that can be obtained by the student through his self-study materials, although some class time is usually given over to the clarification of concepts the student has not grasped through his home study.

Programmed instruction is by itself a useful and efficient tool because, by its emphasis on the clarification of objectives, the student is consciously aware of where he is going and the teacher is forced to clarify his own outlook and objectives. By having known objectives from the outset, the student does not have to become involved in courses in which the objectives are not of his choosing. Programmed instruction is aimed at teaching the student to think and come up with his own interpretation. Kinsler raises the question:

> Is there anything more paternalizing than taking a student to a residence seminary where every aspect of his life is taken care

---

7. James H. Emery, "Bases de Extensión Numero 1: Estudio Propio," *Seminario de Extension,* no. 2 (1971), pp. 1-3.

8. D. Leslie Hill, *Designing a Theological Education by Extension Program: A Philippine Case Study* (South Pasadena, Calif.: William Carey Library, 1974), p. 188.

of every moment of the day. Compare the extension set-up which is so completely deschooled that the professors go to the students, sit down with them in their situation, and discuss their problems as they study theology and carry on the ministry in their churches, and struggle with the needs of their families and communities at the same time.[9]

ADMINISTRATIVE

Goff's third concern is administrative. He charges that theological education has from its origin been in the hands of North American missionaries. This has been especially apparent in the area of establishing curriculum and the preparation of materials. For instance, of the original 34 authors proposed by the Latin American Committee for Theological Texts (CLATT) to produce the Intertexts, only seven were Latin Americans. These authors were to receive orientation from the Advisory Committee for Self-Instructional Texts (CATA). Yet not a single Latin American was among the 15 consultants named to advise the authors and all five of the publishing houses involved in the project were based in the United States. This overwhelming missionary presence was defended at the time on the grounds that the highly trained missionaries were the only people fully capable of such a ministry.[10]

This problem, to which Goff so forcefully called attention, had, however, already been recognized as a problem by both missionaries and nationals involved in the Intertext project. Determined to resolve this problems and encouraged by success of AETTE in Brazil, evangelical leaders who represented programs of theological education by extension in the countries of Spanish-speaking Latin America gathered in Medellín, Colombia, between January 8 and 13 of 1973 to form a Hispanic counterpart of the Brazilian association.

It was at this meeting that the leadership of theological education by extension began to pass into predominantly Latin American hands.

---

9. Kinsler, *op. cit.*
10. Goff, *op. cit.* For an excellent critical summary evaluation of the Intertext project cf. F. Ross Kinsler, "El Pryecto de Intertextos en Español," *Seminario de Extension,* no. 3 (1972), pp. 1-9.

There the Latin American Association of Institutes and Seminaries by Extension (ALISTE) was born. Its purpose is to provide training and orientation to Latin American leadership, promote the interchange of materials and experiences, stimulate the depth and creativity in extension education, and take over the function of CLATT and CATA, both of which ceased to exist at the Medellín meeting, being absorbed into the structure of ALISTE. Initially governed by a predominantly Latin American executive board, ALISTE elected the Rev. José Carrera, veteran Guatemalan pastor and extension educator as president and named national coordinators in 16 countries: 7 missionaries and 9 nationals.

International and interdenominational, a major initial thrust of ALISTE was the development of a four-step project aimed at preparing Latin Americans for leadership in the movement of theological education by extension in Latin America. Sixteen Latin Americans have thus far been prepared during 1974 and 1975. A final group largely embracing nations and denominational groups lacking national leadership will be prepared under the direction of the Evangelical Presbyterian Seminary of Guatemala in collaboration with the Latin American Biblical Seminary, which now offers the world's first Master of Theology degree with specialization in theological education by extension.

At the most recent meeting held in Alajuela, Costa Rica, ALISTE elected a board of directors composed entirely of Latin Americans. A young, though experienced, Ecuadorian, Nelson Castro, fruit of the training project, was elected president. As I listened to the discussion, both formal and informal, which took place during this consultation, I was impressed with the fact that the reins of the movement were passing to a new generation of Latin American leaders. These leaders are convinced of the value of theological education by extension, but also dedicated to subject it to a continuous and serious evaluation in order to insure its scriptural faithfulness, incorporate new advances in educational theory and methodology, develop additional leadership, indigenize and contextualize TEE in accord with the multiple realities and complex necessities of the continent as well as train teachers and writers in each country of Latin America.

STRATEGIC

Another area of crisis in the developing movement, not mentioned by Goff but clearly pointed out by such leaders as Wayne Weld and Peter Savage, has been the need to modify the Guatemalan pattern for lower level students and to explore the possibilities of non-formal education.

TEE for Semi-literate Church Leaders

As originally developed, theological education by extension was predicated on a weekly seminar with students who were capable of working through self-study materials between sessions. An early experiment by George Patterson in Olanchito, Honduras, failed when the rainy season transformed dirt roads into unpassable seas of mud and when semi-literate church leaders were unable to comprehend even the basic materials prepared in Guatemala. Undaunted by initial frustrations and convinced of the validity of the extension concept as a powerful tool for evangelism and church development, Patterson introduced a series of modifications adapting extension methodology to persons of extremely limited education. He introduced change in four areas.

First, he modified the course of study. Evangelism and education were combined. Education became action-oriented and obedience-based, course work serving as a means to the growth of the church rather than an end in itself. Thus, no one learns for the mere sake of learning. Patterson has discovered that the rural person is best motivated when education is functional. For the Christian that means obedience to the Great Commission. There are no diplomas and no one ever graduates. Everyone enrolled is a worker and a student and a teacher at the same time, although those with more experience spend less time in study and more time teaching others. Progress is evaluated by activities, and the purpose of examination is basically diagnostic—to see if the student has understood the lesson. There is no set curriculum. The student studies what he feel he needs to know in order to fulfill his ministry.

Second, he condensed the textbooks. Almost all of Patterson's students were near-subsistence farmers, incapable of studying for long periods of time. He explains:

> Our workers don't read very well. They lack glasses. There is no electricity. There are no newspapers or books in town. They are tired, live among people who don't read, have little practice in reading and possess a limited vocabulary: for this reason they don't like to read. An hour or two of reading a week is all that can be expected.[11]

Finding no materials acceptable for the needs of his semi-literate students, he began preparing his own in order to meet the immediate needs of his students and their churches. The first step was drastic abridgement in length. The next was a drastic reduction in size so that material would fit in a shirt pocket. Then followed a change to a comic strip format, drawn by Patterson himself. The books are brief and interdisciplinary. For instance, one short unit on Augustine combines church history, the doctrine of original sin, and sermon construction. Simple programming is sometimes used, although Patterson has also written an original novel to teach pastoral theology and a poem to tell the history of the Roman Catholic Church in Latin America. A simple, concrete writing style, a single theme, and immediate application are hallmarks of his materials.

Third, he altered the enrollment procedures. Classes were limited to five to help insure discussion rather than lecture. Obedience is the only qualification for entrance. Prospective students must already be active church workers. A new center is not founded unless at least one student is both married and mature. Illiterates are taught to read *after* enrolling. Patterson claims that to date the best teachers in the program have never finished primary school.

Fourth, he changed the teaching methodology. Each class follows a fixed pattern. This includes a report from each student on what he has studied during the past week and what he has accomplished in his ministry. Everyone enters into the discussion about problems encountered in their ministries. Suggestions about possible solutions

---

11. George Patterson, "El Metodo de Extensión Modificado para Uso con Gente de Educación Limitada, *Seminario de Extension,* no. 4 (1972), p. 3. This document is the basic source of information for the description of his program.

are made. The teacher then reviews the diagnostic tests, makes note of progress (students advance at their own rate), and gives out new books according to the need of each student. Then the teacher presents something new—usually something he himself has just studied in his own class with the director of the institute. The class concludes with prayer.

Patterson's ministry with rural persons of limited education provides a model for one possible modification of theological education by extension.

Nonformal Education: The Search for New Alternatives

Another alternative has been the interest of the Latin American Biblical Seminary—particular Professors Rubén Lores, Hugo Zorillo, and Irene Foulkes—in nonformal education. Several models have stimulated their thinking: the Open University in Great Britain; Madrid's University at a Distance; the recognition of up to a year of academic credit for educational experiences secured in a nonformal setting in various educational institutions of the United States such as Adelphia University and Lincoln Open University; the "total language" approach of Costa Rica's Dr. Francisco Gutierrez; the pedagogical impact of Illich and Freire; the investigations of Kinsler and Emery in the field of open education; information about the Union of South Africa's correspondence university, where one can even earn a recognized Ph.D.; the infinite possibility presented by the mass media for theological education; and a variety of other educational experiments in Latin America, particularly in Colombia and Venezuela.

During 1974 the seminary sponsored a workshop on the theme of "Alternatives in Theological Education: Explorations in Nontraditional Education," in order to search further for alternative methods of theological education that would permit men and women to enter into a serious and yet flexible process of theological education.[12] Rubén Lores, recently designated director of the extension department, has presented a project currently under study by the

---

12. C. Hugo Zorilla, ed., *Alternativas en la Educación Teológica: Exploraciones sobre Educacion no-tradicional* (San José, Costa Rica: Seminario Bíblico Latinoamericano, 1975).

faculty and students, to open an international division aimed at providing theological education of the same caliber as that offered in the San José residence program to interested persons without the person's having to leave his or her own locality. Various alternative forms would be employed using local resources in addition to correspondence, tutorials, cassettes, and special projects of investigation.

*   *   *   *   *

Faced with the need to make in-flight corrections, the theological education by extension movement has demonstrated itself capable both of recognizing and modifying its deficiencies, and of making those in-flight corrections. Its flexibility and continued growth justify the optimistic critique offered by the Theological Education Fund:

> In short, extension methods appear as one of the more vital new alternatives for theological education developed in recent years. It seems to offer great potential for many Third World situations. Its potential needs to be fully explored without succumbing to an uncritical eulogy or an angry rejection of its methods.[13]

---

13. Theological Education Fund Staff, "Theological Education by Extension: A Critique of Its Development and Method," *Ministry in Context: The Third Mandate Programme of the Theological Education Fund (1970–77)* (Bromley, Kent, England: The Theological Educational Fund) p. 41.

Part III

Adventure in Theological Education:
A Honduran Case Study

Chapter VIII

SURVEYING THE FIELD

The book of the Acts of the Apostles, a thoroughly researched historical work,[1] contains four sections written in the subjective first person.[2] These four "we sections," as scholars call them, add an element of first-hand testimony to Luke's historical work. In a similar sense, this chapter is a highly subjective, first-person account of the events which took place in the field of theological education in the Evangelical and Reformed Church of Honduras during 1967–70. This case is raw material—the chronological record of one of the earliest attempts to respond to a concrete situation in Latin America by employing extension concepts as part of a comprehensive program of theological education.

In no sense is this case study to be regarded as normative. It is descriptive and suggestive. It invites the reader to compare previously expounded theory and history with practice; to draw parallels to his own situation, to sort out and analyze crucial factors; to note and avoid my errors; to sense the excitement and grapple with the problems of theological education; and finally to seek ever more effective ways to train God's people for the work of ministry. I leave to later historians to objectify, "for we cannot but speak of what we have seen and heard."[3]

---

1. William Barclay, *The Daily Study Bible: The Acts of the Apostles*, p. xix. He concludes: "When we read Acts we may be quite sure that no historian ever had better sources and no historian ever used his sources more accurately and more honestly."
2. The "we" passages are Acts 16:10-17; 20:5-16; 21:1-18; and 27:1–28:16.
3. Acts 4:20.

The work of the Evangelical and Reformed Church is confined to the northwest sector of Honduras—precisely that part of the nation most battered by Hurricane "Fifi" during 1974.

There, in 1967, about 1,000 members and 3,800 Sunday school pupils were organized into 18 congregations and served by 14 full-time pastors. The center of the work is San Pedro Sula, a burgeoning commercial hub of nearly 125,000 inhabitants located in the steaming, fertile Sula Valley, where cattle, sugar cane, bananas, and increasing light industry form the backbone of the economy. The Sula Valley is, in turn, bordered on the north by the Gulf of Mexico and ringed on the other three sides by mountains which someone once described as resembling "a box of ice cream cones turned upside down."

In addition to strong urban congregations in San Pedro Sula, healthy E. & R. congregations are located in the coastal city of Puerto Cortés, the banana company town of La Lima, the mountainous department capital of Yoro, and the bustling commercial center of El Progreso. Several small congregations and numerous preaching points are scattered throughout small rural towns in the valley and tiny rural villages that dot the scenic mountains where the population ekes out a living in lumbering, raising cattle, mining, and subsistence agriculture. Many move to San Pedro Sula in search of a better life.

In cooperation with the United Church Board for World Ministries the E. & R. church carries on extensive educational, medical, agricultural, literature, and communications ministries.

Honduras is one of the poorest nations in Latin America in terms of per capita income. Poverty is omnipresent, especially in the rural areas. In 1960, President Villeda Morales referred to Honduras as the country of the four seventies: 70 percent of the population rural, 70 percent of births illegitimate, 70 percent of the citizens unable to read or write, and 70 percent of the deaths preventable. The average life span is barely 50 years.

In 1967, Honduras had only about 200 miles of paved roads in the entire country, a nation about the size of Tennessee. There are 180 miles separating San Pedro Sula from the national capital and cultural center, Tegucigalpa. It sometimes took as long as 12 hours to travel between the two cities over the unpaved, twisting mountain roads. Although railroads are found only along the coast, domestic air service to almost any part of the country is excellent. The geographical isolation resulting from the poor transportation has given rise to strong regional loyalties. Until the 1969 war with El Salvador, national unity was weak. Instability has long been a hallmark of Honduran politics. A corrupt though not oppressive military dictatorship holds power tightly in its grip behind a façade of apparently democratic institutions. The country has averaged nearly one revolution every two years since its independence from Spain in 1821. Once a cradle of Mayan civilization, Honduras is now largely meztiso—a mixture of Indian and Spanish. A few scattered Indians remain in isolated areas, and many blacks are found along the Atlantic Coast.

BEGINNINGS

In response to a request by Honduran businessman Ramon Guzmán, Sr., the Foreign Mission Board of the Evangelical Synod of North America began missionary work on the northwest coast of Honduras in 1921. The stated aim of the work was personal regeneration by means of the proclamation of the Gospel and social regeneration through the formation of a middle class by means of education. Work expanded to include the departments of Cortés, Yoro, and Santa Barbara, but for years progress was slow. Although a primary school was begun almost at once and efforts at evangelism were intensive, five years passed before the first convert was baptized. Despite slow growth, the missionaries realized that the formation of a self-governing, self-propagating, self-supporting church depended to a large extent on the development of national leadership. They also believed that it was better to train their own leadership than to call leadership from other denominations or train men outside of Honduras.

Thus, in 1934, the Evangelical Theological Seminary was established in Pinalejo, Santa Barbara, by the late Rev. Walter Herrscher. Not only was Herrscher the lone professor, but he also was pastor of a church, directed a primary school, and evangelized the surrounding area while his wife taught in the school and established a small clinic. The predominant pattern of theological education was apprenticeship. Students followed Herrscher in his travels and visitation, read the books he suggested, conversed at length with him, and under his watchful supervision practiced what he taught them.

With the passing of the years, instruction became more formal as seminary enrollment climbed to four, five, or six full-time students. They attended regular morning classes and completed definite assignments in addition to assisting in the Pinalejo congregation and evangelizing the surrounding villages. The seminary passed from being basically an apprenticeship system to a "school of the prophets" in the early New England sense. Six grades, then nine, were required before Herrscher would accept a student for study. In addition to the students from the sponsoring Evangelical Mission, other groups, particularly the Moravians, sometimes sent students. Until Herrscher's sudden death in 1957, 15 men had studied under him, of whom five are still active pastors in the Evangelical and Reformed Church.

Upon Herrscher's death the seminary moved to El Progreso, where three students came under the tutelage of the Rev. Maurice Reidesel, an apt teacher with strong Calvinist convictions. Reidesel, an active evangelist and church planter, resigned from the Mission board two years later in protest over what he considered creeping liberalism within the newly founded United Church of Christ. Thus, for three years there was no institution for theological education among the Evangelical and Reformed Church of Honduras. Reidesel's three students were given the status of "workers" and assigned to care for local congregations.

With no formal training institution of their own, the church leadership now looked to international training institutions. Two students went to Guatemala to study. Also an interest in continuing education sprouted. Scholarships were offered for an additional year of training to experienced pastors. This training was to be taken outside of Honduras in order to amplify the field of vision of Honduran pastoral leadership and foment an influx of new ideas.

In 1962, after a sudden spurt of growth in church membership, the

Rev. Kenneth Daniel Sell led in establishing a theological institute in the north coast city of San Pedro Sula. Entrance requirements were set at sixth grade with hope of raising them to ninth grade within three years and full secondary level after another three years. Students were to be received every three years at the beginning, with hopes of taking in a new class each year if the institute grew. Sell was the only full-time professor, but he did an excellent job by using capable nationals and missionaries as part-time teachers. He began a formal library, established a clear-cut constitution, and organized a supervised field-work system. In fact, in nearly all its aspects, the new Theological Institute was a very commendable though modest model of Eden or Lancaster Theological Seminary. Five students were initially received, of which one was dismissed shortly thereafter for irresponsibility.

At that point, theological education was largely limited to the residence program. The theological institute was seen as the place where students went to prepare themselves to become full-time pastors. Efforts at leadership training during this era appear disjointed and lacking in coordination.

In 1965, a new class of five students was received, including two women who enrolled in the newly initiated program of Christian Education under the capable direction of Mrs. Betty Sell. However, that same year dissension beween the Board and missionary personnel as well as among the missionaries themselves led to the resignation of the Sells. The rectorship passed to John Will.

Will proved to be an amazing missionary. Gifted with linguistic ability, he mastered Spanish, according to the nationals, within a year of arriving on the field better than any other missionary in the history of the mission. Extremely neat, disciplined, and efficient by nature, he had an undergraduate engineering degree plus experience in the armd services; his administrative and artistic talents were developed to a high degree. First in his graduating class at Eden Seminary, he brought academic competence to the position. His cooperation with the churches during the Evangelism-in-Depth campaign in Honduras and his own profound religious experience endeared him to the national church and gained public confidence on behalf of the struggling

Theological Institute by those nationals suspicious of liberal theology among the younger missionaries.

Unfortunately, he determined that he would not return to Honduras after furlough, in protest at the recall of Elmer Gumper by the United Church Board for World Ministries. Prior to his furlough date he made application to the U.S. State Department for a foreign service appointment. When the appointment came through sooner than expected, he resigned his position before finishing his first term on the field.

During the rectorship of Will, the Theological Institute joined the newly formed Latin American Association of Biblical and Theological Institutions (ALIBT), which later developed into ALET. This happy decision provided a constant source of new ideas and helpful approaches for training the ministry.

The Rev. J. Kenneth Trauger became the third rector for the same group of students. He was called from his task of rural evangelism and lay training in the Department of Yoro in order to finish the second year of the cycle and to serve until I arrived from language school in August of 1967.

At this moment the Synod decided to enroll an additional two workers who had begun but never completed their education in Progreso ten years previously. Despite their years of service they were not eligible for ordination because they had never had the opportunity to finish their third year of theological training.

NEW DIRECTIONS

Ken Trauger was a hard worker. Also, he brought with him into the rectorship several key assets that his more academically oriented predecessors had lacked: he had a vision of total theological education and an intense love for the development of the rural as well as the urban church.

In addition to administering the residence program during an interim year and considerably building up the library, Trauger made two significant contributions which in reality laid the groundwork for the changes which took place during the following year.

First, while serving as a rural evangelist in Yoro, Trauger became concerned over the lack of pastoral care in the rural churches, in part due to the failure of Synod to recognize and train the natural leaders of the rural communities. In 1966, he organized and directed a ten-week course for laymen, who after training would work under pastors of larger charges, but who would actually be the leaders of the congregations where they resided—teaching, preaching, and counseling. Seven persons attended the entire course—two of whom continue as very active and two as moderately active leaders. Follow-up was to take the form of quarterly seminars and attendance at the monthly pastors meetings.

However, the ten-week institute had proven too long and eliminated many who could benefit. On the other hand, the short-term institutes used in the past had not been long enough to effectively train rural leaders. A middle way had to be found and no one was more conscious of this than Trauger.

While I was in language school in Costa Rica, I became aware of the extensive correspondence courses of the Latin America Mission. Seeing in these courses a possible source of study for low-level leadership training courses, I carried a set of twelve texts to Honduras during an orientation trip in May, 1967. As a result of discussions during that week and further correspondence, it was decided to use the LAM correspondence courses as the curriculum for the training of the lay pastors.

Five courses would be taught during a month-long short-term institute held in one of the rural congregations at one end of the Evangelical and Reformed zone of work. Courses on Introduction to the Bible, Personal Evangelism, New Testament Introduction, Basic Doctrine, and Homiletics were to be offered to those candidates approved by their congregations. Three more courses: Epistles of Paul, Introduction to the Old Testament, and Prophets and Poetry of the Old Testament were to be completed by correspondence during the following 11 months, with Trauger making quarterly visits to each of the students to tutor and encourage them.

The following year there was again to be a short-term institute, this time at the other end of the Evangelical and Reformed zone, in order to complete four more courses: Christian Education, Theology,

Romanism, and the Sects. The previously mentioned courses were to be supplemented with special short courses on such themes as Bible Distribution, Music, Hygiene, Church Administration, Functioning of the Consistory, and Stewardship. During the month-long institutes themselves, filmstrips were to be shown nightly.

The students took turns leading daily worship and Bible study. On weekends they went out in teams of four for practical work. Those students who completed their courses received their certificates of graduation from the Latin American Biblical Seminary Correspondence Division during the regular November graduation exercises of the Theological Institute.

Even though this training program was to be a part of the total program of the Theological Institute, Trauger was named to be the director of the lower-level program responsible to the Council of the Theological Institute. The revamped program was scheduled to go into effect in August, 1968, a month after the Traugers' return to the field following furlough.

Unfortunately, this program failed to mushroom as expected, even though enthusiasm among laymen was high and the institutes themselves came off quite well. Trauger, rightly I believe, attributes the failure to the indifference of Synod leaders who had no Synod funds invested and to some pastors who saw these popular lay leaders as threats to their authoritarian stance.

Second, through a visit to Guatemala, Trauger came into contact with theological education by extension while it was still in its early stages of development. Shortly afterward, in response to requests from laymen in San Pedro Sula for more advanced theological training, he organized an extension center in San Pedro Sula to function on a trial basis during the first quarter of 1967. In addition to the five residence students who were required to take the course, 20 laymen responded to the 13-week pilot project.

Unfortunately, the course selected by chance was an advanced historical theology course and proved too difficult for the neophyte theological students. All but one of the laymen dropped out. The course itself was intended to be taught over an entire year. It was simply too concentrated. Trauger's initial effort was to be characteristic of the hit and miss efforts of the next couple of years.

However, the one thing of value that was proven was that there were laymen who wanted to study their faith seriously. It also indicated that the recommendations of the Guatemalan Seminary about the use of its materials be taken seriously.

Chapter IX

CHARTING THE COURSE: 1967

On August 19, 1967, eleven days after the Traugers left for furlough, we arrived in steaming San Pedro Sula, prepared to cultivate
the germinating plans sown by Ken Trauger.

Two days after arrival, I assumed the rectorship of the Theological
Institute, the fourth rector in less than three years. My initial responsibilities included teaching courses on "World Mission" and "A
Christian View of Communism," maintaining the library, and super-
vising the student field work. Five students were in their final quarter
of studies preceding graduation.

A few days after arrival in Honduras, I received a letter inviting
me to attend the now-famous workshop in Armenia, Colombia. But
not realizing the significance of this gathering, being acquainted with
the movement toward theological education by extension only at the
functional level, feeling very inadequate as a theological professor,
and still lacking fluency in Spanish, I declined the invitation. Although a wise decision in the short run, it significantly set back our
own extension program, which tended to develop on a hit or miss
basis without a truly solid theoretical framework.

In preparation for the missions course, I read extensively in the
works of Roland Allen and Donald McGavran. This experience
radically altered my thinking. My previous idea of theological education revolved around the training of promising young men for
future service, with graduation from an institutional theological residence program as the correct road to ordination. Allen taught me
the significance of selecting and training mature natural leaders,
through his emphasis that it is easier to add training to gifts than gifts
to training. McGavran showed me the importance of giving priority

to church planting and development in missionary strategy.[1] He also provided me with tools to analyze the situation in which I was working. His many illustrations reflected to me the reality of what I was experiencing—seeing, hearing, doing—in Honduras. I began to catch a vision of the value of the tent-making ministry and the various options in regard to ministerial support. I did not yet know what to do with all of these new ideas. But I knew that they corresponded to the reality I was experiencing. During my years in Honduras I turned again and again to the writings of these two men for guidance, inspiration, and food for thought.

At the close of 1967, a number of crucial steps were taken by the Theological Institute which were to determine the course we were to follow during the next few years.

First, we took tentative steps toward organizing an extension program to begin functioning at the beginning of the 1970 school year. Although I began to make tentative plans toward the establishment of an extension program, I was convinced that I needed to observe firsthand the Guatemalan model. However, other responsibilities made such a trip impossible until early January, 1968.

We planned to organize one center in either Puerto Cortes or El Progreso, purposely bypassing San Pedro Sula. However, initial interest ran so high at both Puerto Cortes and El Progreso, that we decided to begin with both centers.

Second, a proposal from the Methodist Theological Seminary—up to that time the School for the Preparation of Methodist Workers (EPOM)—of Alajuela, Costa Rica, to collaborate in the formation of an upper level (secondary education required) theological school on a truly interdenominational basis for Central America was rejected by the Council of the Theological Institute.

The Board of the Theological Institute in Honduras reacted by defining their own position: they favored the establishment of a single theological school on an interdenominational basis in Honduras. They

---

1. A personal research project revealed that all of the existing congregations of the Evangelical and Reformed Church in Honduras had been founded by missionaries and that no graduate of our Theological Institute going back to 1935 had ever founded a single congregation.

believed that the differences among Central American nations were as great as the differences between Central America and South America. Besides, they added, it was best to train students in the environment where they would be working. Furthermore, there was no faculty member that could be loaned to Costa Rica, nor were there enough upper-level candidates to merit involvement in such a project.

The dream of a united training school for Honduras has never been realized because of the strong regionalism in the country.

While the possibility of forming a single residence school in Tegucigalpa, with a network of extension centers throughout the country, was not propitious in 1968, it had become so by 1970. During the intervening years there had been some informal conversation along this line among such groups as the Evangelical and Reformed Church, the Conservative Baptists, the Moravians, the Mennonites, the United Brethren, the World Gospel Mission, and the Friends. But a possible interdenominational consultation slated for La Ceiba in September, 1970, failed to materialize. Such a step, if pursued, could revolutionize theological education and serve as a great unifying factor on the Honduran scene. Still another possibility would be for the Evangelical Presbyterian Seminary of Guatemala to expand to establish a network of centers throughout all of Central America.

Third, a system of multi-level theological education was established. This sprang out of the realization that the differing levels of education among the leadership of the Evangelical and Reformed Church of Honduras called for a comprehensive program of theological education adapted to the level of the students.[2] Even though some such programs existed they tended to be disjointed and fragmented: residential theological education was under the Board of the Theological Institute, sabbatical scholarships were under the control of the Executive Committee of Synod, lay leadership was under the authority of an individual missionary, with no provision for scholarship

2. A. Clark Scanlon, *Church Growth through Theological Education* (Eugene, Ore.: Institute of Church Growth, 1962), p. 33. What Scanlon points out about Guatemala is also true of Honduras. There is a demand for various levels of leadership.

aid to qualified students to study in one of the interdenominational centers outside of Honduras.

The final shape of our attempt at comprehensive multi-level, theological education assumed the following shape:

1. SABBATICAL: Pastors who had served ten years or more in the parish were eligible for a year of subsidized study in an area which would contribute to their effectiveness as a parish pastor. Pastors were to be encouraged to study outside of Honduras, to enlarge their vision of the work and to observe new models. While this program had existed since the late 1950's, it had never before been coordinated under the Board of the Theological Institute.

2. SCHOLARSHIP: Scholarships were to be made available to students who had completed their secondary education and who wished to prepare themselves for a full-time church vocation. They were to be granted a scholarship equal to the cost of educating them at the Theological Institute in San Pedro Sula. This constituted a major breakthrough. Up to that time Synod had tried to force all candidates to attend the Theological Institute, and any student who went to study elsewhere was looked upon as a renegade preparing himself against the will of Synod, usually at the expense of a sympathetic missionary. Re-enry problems were thereby multiplied.

3. RESIDENCE: The existing residence program was continued. Students who had completed their primary education were awarded a Diploma in Theology upon the successful completion of three years of studies at the Institute. A class was to be received once every three years. It was to complete its cycle of studies before another class was to be received. Plans were made to upgrade the residence program so that by 1973 the minimum level for entrance would be the completion of ninth grade. Those who entered with this background would work toward a *Bachillerato en Teología,* a professional degree in theology.

4. EXTENSION: This new approach was a means to extend the outreach of the Theological Institute through decentralized theological education. By its very nature the extension system was multi-level, embracing those studying for the Diploma, *Bachillerato,* or *Licenciatura.* Whereas the residence program was to be upgraded thus,

the route to ordination through extension education was to be left open to persons with only a primary education at all times. The program of studies was to be the same in residence as in extension, although the student could progress at his own rate through the extension system—taking up to 15 years to complete his studies. The extension system also opened the door for the theological education of laymen who could not possibly study in a daytime residence program.

5. CORRESPONDENCE: Also termed the lay minister program was the low-level program. This arm of the comprehensive program of theological education was aimed at literate persons who had not finished primary school. As previously mentioned, it was carried on through a short-term institute of one month. This was followed up by correspondence studies throughout the year. The course was completed by a second month-long institute the following year. Twelve subjects were studied. The examinations were corrected in Costa Rica. Students who completed the program were awarded the Certificate and were eligible to become lay ministers—a kind of second-class ordained clergy.

6. CONTINUING EDUCATION: The one missing link is a program of continuing education for pastors who do not go on sabbaticals. Originally, it was hoped that some pastors would enter the extension program either for their personal enrichment, or to upgrade their present theological degree. As it turned out, only one pastor (who had earned a Diploma at the old Pinalejo Seminary and had since finished his secondary education) entered the extension program to upgrade his diploma. But this did not take place until 1970. One pastor did begin to audit classes, but when I made the mistake of calling upon him to answer a question on biblical content which he was unable to answer, he was so ashamed before the laymen in the class, that he never again appeared in the classroom. Effective strides toward a program on continuing education were not made until 1970.

Our program of theological education aimed at comprehensiveness. We recognized the need for different levels of leadership: well-educated leaders for urban areas, where cultural and economic stand-

Diagram F: Multi-level Theological Education in Honduras

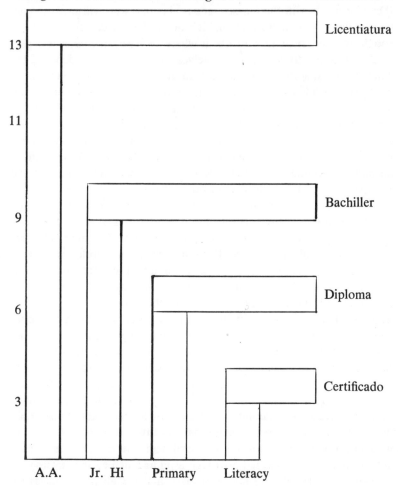

Vertical bars—Pre-theological level of secular studies
Horizontal bars—Theological studies (equivalent of three years, but
  longer bars mean generally more extensive studies)

Adapted from Ralph D. Winter, "Introduction," *Theological Education by
Extension*, p. 383.

ards were high; pastors whose standard of living and education fit them for work with the masses; unpaid laymen who will provide vital leadership in the local church. Through theological education we sought to encourage all students at whatever level, in whatever aspect of the program, to consider themselves as full-fledged students of the Theological Institute. We sought to make this more concrete by inviting all students not only to the annual closing convocation, but also to any pertinent workshops or lecture series which the Theological Institute might sponsor. See Diagram F.

Of decisive importance for moving in the direction we had chosen was a trip I took to Guatemala in late December of 1967 enroute to an annual meeting of the Latin American Association of Theological Schools (ALET) held in Cuernavaca, Mexico.

A few days prior to the trip, Dr. and Mrs. Alfred Carlton visited San Pedro Sula enroute back to the United States after visiting relatives in Managua, Nicaragua. Dr. Carlton was at that time executive vice-president of the United Church Board for World Ministries. While in Honduras, he expressed the opinion that the direction that our program of theological education ought to assume, "the priority posture," was the upgrading of our residence program so as to train pastors capable of ministering to the true decision makers in the upper classes of Honduras. At one time I would have given wholehearted assent to that idea, but my experience and reading was causing me to raise questions precisely because the highly trained pastors envisioned by Dr. Carlton could not be supported by our congregations. The decision-making upper classes were not in our churches; and it is likely that they could be influenced more by a Protestant laymen than by a pastor. Also, highly trained pastors often proved ineffective in identifying with the poor in the rural and the urban areas. Five consecutive persons trained on a high level in four key seminaries outside of Honduras during the previous years had all failed miserably as pastors. The people of Honduras were not asking the questions these men were trained to answer, and the very atmosphere of their training made them incapable of identifying socially with the persons they were being trained to serve. Two have since emigrated to the United States; one of the remaining three is a teacher, one is a businessman, and the other is a teacher in an evangelical high school, where he functions effectively within the structure of an academic setting.

During the trip to Guatemala, I was privileged to spend two days with F. Ross Kinsler: a morning with him at an extension class, and a day with him at the seminary going over the teaching materials and absorbing as much about the operation of an extension system as possible. I departed for Mexico with my briefcase filled with documents and other materials concerning theological education by extension.

The meeting at Cuernavaca had three high points for me. First was the immense wealth of experience, coupled with a keen perspective, in the person of John Mackay. His lectures and conversations were a vast source of wisdom and inspiration for viewing things in the context of the Latin American reality. The second high point was the discussions which had direct bearing upon theological education, particularly those which zeroed in on the acknowledged problem of "re-entry" faced by graduates of theological institutions after three years of extraction from their natural cultural group. Theological education by extension was discussed a great deal. I remember spending four hours in discussion with Ralph Winter—or should I say listening to Winter talk? I was amazed and impressed at the tremendous range of his ideas, his powers of both analysis and synthesis, and his creativity. Of special interest to me was his analysis of theological education by extension from an anthropological point of view. A final high point was my own rather surprising election as treasurer of ALET, considering that I was nominated from the floor rather than by the nominating committee and was the only North American on the six-man executive committee. The contacts which grew out of this responsibility during the next three years were invaluable in providing resources for our program of theological education in Honduras.

Chapter X

A YEAR OF EXPERIMENTATION: 1968

Arriving back in Honduras in mid-January, I renewed contact with the pastors at Puerto Cortes and El Progreso. They assured me that everything was ready to begin and that enthusiasm was running high. Although we had originally planned to bypass San Pedro Sula so that time would erase the memory of the collapse of the experimental center there the previous year, one of the laymen insisted on having a center in San Pedro Sula. He had been in the course offered the previous year and although he had not completed all requirements, he came closest among the 20 laymen. A prospective residence student with a large family said he could not afford to quit his job, move to the city, and support his family on the scholarship offered him. He requested the opportunity to study by extension at a San Pedro Sula center. A third student, a government engineer in charge of the national electric company in northern Honduras, indicated his interest in serious theological study. Another student, also an engineer, began studies, but he had to discontinue them when he was transferred to another part of the country. Late in the year a fifth student joined the San Pedro Sula center, but later decided that before he took any more theological studies he was going to finish high school, and that was going to take him the next five years!

By mid-February centers were functioning in three cities: Puerto Cortes, El Progreso, and San Pedro Sula. A course in the inductive study of the Gospel of Mark was offered. For the advanced students the study was to include a survey of the life and teachings of Jesus.

PUERTO CORTES

The Puerto Cortes center met each Friday evening. Initial enthusiasm ran high. About 25 students began the year. All students were at the diploma level. However, it soon became apparent that difficulties were present. The pastor, in his desire to have a large group, had encouraged people barely literate to participate. Many others with the minimum requirements were not able to receive the individual help they needed to develop disciplined study habits. Still others did not realize the seriousness of the demands laid upon them as theological students. While the minimum age level for extension students had been set at 16, two years lower than the requirement for residence study, the pastor had enrolled some 15-year-olds and one 14-year-old. Added to that, my Spanish was not yet fluent. While there were no serious communication barriers that I could detect, there was some occasional static.

The result was that after the first examination the number of participants dropped quickly to about a dozen students, the majority of whom with increasing seriousness went on to complete the year and form the nucleus of the group for the next two years.

At the same time, I discovered that for meaningful class discussion it was impossible to allow each student to progress at his own speed and found it necessary to pace the class with regular weekly assignments. Class sessions consisted basically of a review of the assignment followed by a discussion of questions raised by the students or by me along with an application of the lessons to the contemporary scene in the life of the student, his church and the world. Since our only possible classroom was the church sanctuary, we arranged the pews in a double semicircle to aid discussion. Note-taking was difficult in those circumstances, and we had to compete with traffic noise from a busy highway.

Despite my early elation at the size and interest of the group, followed by shock and disappointment at its rapid dwindling, I saw the dozen who remained begin to develop an *esprit de corps* that manifested itself in an increased enthusiasm both in routine church responsibilities and outreach activities. Branch Sunday schools took on new life. The content of Sunday school lessons and Christian Endeavor talks improved. Students began to feel comfortable leading worship and even delivered the message on "Theological Institute Day."

EL PROGRESO

The El Progreso center met each Thursday evening in the parish primary school. We began with 13 persons, three of whom were lost very early in the year by moving to towns beyond the reach of the center. The majority of the students were young single women teachers, *bachillerato*-level students. In a fairly short time we lost the diploma-level students and remained with the five upper-level students. They did high quality work. Three of them, teachers in the Evangelical and Reformed primary school system, said that the course helped them greatly in teaching the Bible classes for which they were responsible. As the year progressed, it became increasingly apparent to me that these persons were doing work of superior quality to those in the residence program. Since this was also happening in the center located in San Pedro Sula, I saw the possibilities of reaching not only *down* with theological education to the rural under-privileged, but also *up* to the professional people whom Dr. Carlton had spoken of reaching through upgrading our residence program. Through extension, our theological education was being upgraded by the presence of students who were *already* of the professional class.

Meeting in the classroom of the primary school, we fought bad lighting and occasional tarantulas which crawled on the damp whitewashed walls in the evening. And by keeping a Coleman lamp handy we survived both burned-out fluorescent lights and the frequent power failures of the erratic city power plant.

While visiting the Sunday school at El Progreso the following year, I was impressed at the lesson one of the students taught—the international lessons for that quarter consisting of a study of the Gospel of Mark—and the way she was able to utilize much of what she learned in both methodology and content from the study of the previous year.

SAN PEDRO SULA

In San Pedro Sula, where the group met each Monday evening, a unique situation developed. Whereas the Puerto Cortés group was a mixed group of youth all on the diploma level and the El Progreso group was composed of *bachillerato*-level professional women, the

San Pedro group was made up of males on all three levels, with one student in his twenties, another in his thirties, and one in his forties. It was here that I saw demonstrated the effectiveness of the multi-level principle of theological education.

The university-educated student tended to think abstractly, and the diploma-level student was constantly bringing him down to earth with the insistence that he express himself in simple langauage. Yet as the year progressed I could see growth in the lower-level student as he learned from the wider experiences of his more-traveled and better-read fellow-students. There were no dropouts except for one university-level engineer who began two weeks late and had to drop out soon afterward because of a transfer to a different job. Fellowship was intense and the quality of work high.

The class lasted two hours. The following morning from 7:00 to 8:00 the telegraph operator studied homiletics with me in a tutoring relationship using extension materials. Thus, by the end of the year he had completed two courses. A year later he was preaching regularly in the small village where he resided. Unfortunately the pastor, a recent graduate from the residence program, saw the developing layman as a threat. This caused a head-on clash, which was solved by moving the pastor and leaving the layman in charge.

EVALUATION

That year I finished the term with a case of hepatitis. The students assumed responsibility for carrying out the first end-of-the-year convocation ever held without a graduation. Prof. Victor Monterroso's convocation address before several hundred people in Central Church was on the theme of the relationship of Theological Education to Church Growth. A co-author of *Latin-American Church Growth,* he also led a workshop aimed at enlarging the horizons of the students by helping them to see their own church in the context of the entire Protestant movement in Latin America.

The year finished with student morale very high, but there were problems as well as victories, as I pointed out in my annual reports to Synod and to the Mission Board.

Viewed positively:

This year we put into operation a full five division multi-level program of theological education. About 50 persons are participating in the program from those who have completed only first grade to a university graduate; from humble maid, laborers, and farmers to business and professional people. This has been a year of expansion and experimentation whereby we have truly sought to make theological education the servant of the church.[1]

The 50 students included the lower-level correspondence students. Among the extension students, 16 of them had completed a total of 162 quarter hours.

My report to Synod also detailed some of the problems we encountered.

Although I consider this a good number (fifteen completed at least one full course), we ought to consider that many left off studying during the year. Before the first test there were almost 30 in Puerto Cortés, 11 in El Progreso, and always the three in San Pedro. I don't know all the factors. I suppose that among these factors would be included the lack of academic preparation in the primary school, the lack of desire to really study, false understanding of the nature of the course, lack of experience and ability of the professor, the barrier of language, interruptions because of the program of the church, etc. Nevertheless, there is now a nucleus in each center. Furthermore, there is not much shame involved in leaving the classes as if one were a student in the residence plan.[2]

I also made three recommendations at the end of the report: stand firm in accepting no one who is not at least 16 years of age and a primary school graduate; ask pastors to inspire the real leaders of their congregations to matriculate; limit the number of students in each center to 12.

---

1. Kenneth and Ann Mulholland, "Annual Report—1968," p. 1. Unpublished report.

2. Kenneth Mulholland, "Informe del Instituto Teologico Preparado para la XVIII Asamblea General del Sinodo de la Iglesia Evangelica y Reformada de Honduras," p. 3. Unpublished report dated November, 1968. (The translation of this unpublished report is made by this writer, as are all subsequent translations of Spanish documents included in this chapter.)

Chapter XI

A YEAR OF CONSOLIDATION: 1969

Personal illness interrupted the smooth flow of operations in the first days of 1969, as both my wife, Ann, and I fell sick.

THE ALET DEBATE

Nevertheless, my health had improved sufficiently by the end of January, 1969, to attend the annual ALET meeting at the Baptist Theological Institute in Managua, Nicaragua. A workshop was not scheduled along with the meeting. Instead, the merits of theological education by extension were discussed in a paper prepared by Prof. James Emery of the Evangelical Presbyterian Seminary of Guatemala. Those chosen to react to the paper included such diverse persons as José Arreguin, dean of the Baptist Theological Seminary of Mexico; Jacinto Ordoñez, dean of the Methodist Theological Seminary of Costa Rica and executive secretary of ALET; Prof. Louis Weil of the Episcopal Seminary of Puerto Rico; and Prof. Charles Vore, director of the Berea Bible Institute of the Friends Mission in Guatemala.

Although Emery concluded that the traditional and the extension seminaries were in reality supplementary and therefore ought to be friends, the body of his lecture was a strong statement of the affirmative case for extension:

> The question continually comes up. Do you expect the extension seminary to displace the traditional one? The question carries a heavy emotional load, especially when it casts a shadow over heavy investments in buildings, professors, etc., who feel threatened by any radical change. In this sense I do not believe that the extension seminary itself poses a threat, but simply calls attention to the direction of movement in the present day evan-

gelical churches. If the traditional seminary is replaced, it will be because its ties with tradition are so great that it cannot modify its program in such a way as to meet the present day needs and challenges of the church and society.[1]

After making comparisons between the two systems in pre-service and in-service training, educational purpose, and internal efficiency, Emery concluded:

> Many pastors, however, are not conscious of what is going on around them. The seminary must shake off whatever traditions that prevent it from training pastors in such a way that they will be able responsibly and effectively to guide the man on the street. It seems to me that the extension seminary can provide such training because it makes for flexible patterns of ministry and challenges pastors to think and act in new paths. By this we do not say that the traditional institution has no role to play, though I believe that the traditional seminary will have to undergo changes to face the new challenges. But the two systems of ministerial training can co-exist, but probably both will have to constantly be open to change.[2]

The rejoinders displayed the variety of attitudes toward extension: Arreguin bitterly defended the traditional system; Ordoñez allowed that extension was good for laymen and as pre-residence study, but not adequate for first-class theological education; Weil appeared indifferent, failing to speak to the issues raised; and Vore's reply, though superficial, supported Emery.

Unfortunately I was unable to arrive on time and missed the debate, although I was present for the entire business meeting. However, Gregorio Romero, pastor of First Evangelical and Reformed Church, San Pedro Sula, went ahead as delegate of the Theological Institute and did get into the debate. Later he requested that we establish an urban center for the correspondence course in First Church, covering a lesson each week for three years. His interest sparked some support in Honduras among noninvolved pastors in favor of theological education by extension.

---

1. James Emery, "The Traditional and Extension Seminary: Conflict or Cooperation—Friends or Enemies," *Theological Education by Extension,* pp. 219-220.
2. *Ibid.,* p. 230.

The fact that I was assigned a room with Ordoñez, adjoining the room where Emery stayed, enabled me to become involved in the discussion and the interchange that resulted from Emery's presentation. During the meeting, I was re-elected treasurer for two more years, thus enabling me to continue valuable international contacts with extension leaders.

A CURRICULUM ESTABLISHED

Between the 1968 and 1969 school years, the Board of the Theological Institute had been struggling with the development of a new unified curriculum which would serve both extension and residence programs. Already the same texts were being utilized where this was feasible.

The residence program used the quarter system and was based on having the student carry two subjects each term in each of the three following departments, Bible, Church, and Ministry; plus one or two "secular" subjects, i.e., Spanish, typing, first aid, literacy education, etc. After much thinking and struggling, it was finally decided that the extension and future residence programs would consist of 15 one-year courses equally distributed among three fields: Bible, Church Life and Thought, and Ministry.

The philosophy of the Bible Department was to give a broad overview of the entire Bible with more detailed study of the more important sections. Opportunity would be given for careful inductive analysis of three key biblical books representing different literary types in the belief that the principles learned could be carried over into the personal study of other books. Courses included Old Testament survey, life and teachings of Jesus with an inductive study of Mark, life and letters of Paul with an inductive study of Romans.

The emphasis of the Department of Church Life and Thought was to show the inter-relation of the life and thought of the church through the ages as well as in contemporary Latin America, to enable the student to understand and express the central affirmations of Protestant Christianity both positively and negatively, and to aid the student in the thoughtful application of those affirmations to the contemporary scene morally as well as doctrinally. Courses in this department included church history, systematic theology, historical theology of Protestant Christianity, apologetics, and personal and social ethics.

The Department of Ministry sought to provide students with adequate vehicles for ministry through courses in Christian education, preaching and worship, pastoral counselling, church administration, and communication.

INTEGRATION WITH THE COLEGIO

With a new curriculum approved by the board of the Theological Institute and enthusiastically received by the students, we sought a way to integrate the courses in the Theological Institute with the Bible Department of the Evangelical High School through the extension program.

The specific plan which developed called for the Bible Department of the High School, or *Colegio,* to teach the inductive studies on Jeremiah, Mark and Romans in three-year cycles. Thus, those students who wished to finish their secondary education before beginning theological studies could complete their inductive book studies during their secondary education. By taking one evening class each year, they could finish their secondary education and at the same time complete six of the 15 courses required for their theological degree. In this way they could finish their theological education in only two years of full-time study.

At the same time residence theological students with only a primary education would supplement their theological studies with key secular subjects taken at the high school.

The high school chaplain, the Rev. Arnaldo Evo Rivera, strongly favored the idea because it gave him systematic materials for his Bible classes with which to work. Also, it tied together the Theological Institute and the *Colegio.*

This proposal failed. First, there really were not that many students in the *Colegio* interested in theological studies; only one person followed through on the combined proposed program. Second, the inductive book studies proved too difficult for the high school students who were not highly motivated to do any studying outside of class.

However, on the positive side we did discover the value of inductive study methodology when the Theological Institute students, with only a primary school education—six grades—were not only able to compete with 10th, 11th, and 12th grade college preparatory and normal school students in fields such as education, psychology, and sociology, but were actually able to do superior work. The inductive methodology which we had employed in theological education had taught them how to separate the primary from the secondary, the important from the trivial, in their studies.

One graduate, Santiago Arguijo, while pastoring a thriving local congregation completed two years of high school in a single year. In 14 of the 19 courses he passed, his grades were so high that he was not required to take the government examination. "Impossible!" cried the educational authorities in Tegucigalpa, "there must be some mistake." They immediately launched an investigation. The investigators reported that not only was there no mistake, but Arguijo had indeed passed more courses in a single year than anyone in the previous history of Honduras. Arguijo confided to me in early 1973 that it was the inductive methodology employed in his theological studies that enabled him to accomplish the feat.

THE BETHEL SERIES

Beginning in 1969, we employed the Bethel Series as a means of teaching our Bible survey courses through a pictorial concept approach.

While visiting Mexico City following the ALET meeting at Cuernavaca, I had the privilege of spending time at the Baptist Theological Seminary. There I encountered material from the Bethel Series, about which I had previously read in the March, 1966, edition of *Eternity Magazine*.

This program, developed by the Rev. Harley Swiggum of the Bethel Lutheran Church of Madison, Wisconsin,

> . . . is designed to help adults gain a deeper understanding of the Scriptures by providing them with a sweeping overview of the

major messages of the Old and New Testaments. It uses paintings depicting interrelated biblical ideas to do this.[3]

Swiggum was so enthused with the initial results from the ten pictures he developed to teach basic fundamentals of Christian faith that he went on to prepare an adult study plan for the Old Testament. He reduced to 20 the major categories of study, which he then divided into their simplest fundamentals. He then had paintings designed to communicate these ideas. Later, a New Testament course of study was developed.

The paintings were not esthetically designed to be works of art, but rather visual outlines of thematic biblical truth. For instance,

> The first painting, illustrating the teaching of Genesis 1 and 2 and Psalms 8 and 24, portrays several major concepts relating to creation. For example, there is a pair of hands lifting the earth out of a hazy mist to symbolize that God created the heavens and the earth; and a crown held by the man standing on the earth indicates that man is the crown of creation. Some paintings portray more than a dozen concepts.[4]

In its United States setting, the 28 persons selected out of the gigantic 6,100-member Bethel Lutheran Church spent each Monday night for two years (minus summers) learning not only the content of the Bible, but how to communicate it. Herein lay one of the key principles of the Bethel Series. Each class member had to learn key concepts, and to practice teaching those concepts to others.

> Between class sessions they were required to spend a minimum of seven to ten hours weekly studying Scripture. As a way of learning hundreds of Biblical concepts they were urged to carry study cards with them at all times. . . . The final exam was an essay test which took two hours to complete.[5]

Upon perusing this material for the first time in Mexico, I en-

---

3. W. L. Thorkelsen, "Paintings Teach the Bible in Depth," *Eternity Magazine* XVII (March, 1966), p. 26.

4. *Ibid.,* p. 27.

5. *Ibid.* It is interesting to note that the Lutheran Church in Japan hopes to have 10,000 lay evangelists trained in the Bethel Series by 1976. In addition to Portuguese and Japanese, the material has also been translated into German, Slovak, and Estonian.

visioned its possibilities for Honduras and saw that it might be taught in congregations.

J. Kenneth Trauger, then on furlough, was contacted. The Mission Board granted him permission to attend the two-week summer workshop held in Madison, Wisconsin, in order to receive training. Although the Bethel Series had been translated into Portuguese in order to aid the large Lutheran constituency in Brazil, it had never been translated into Spanish. For this reason, the Theological Institute received permission to conduct a pilot project in Spanish through our extension system. Trauger translated the entire text into Spanish. After revision by a national, it was then mimeographed for distribution and use.

As we opened the 1969 school year with Old Testament survey as the basic course, nearly 50 persons responded; centers were set up in the same places as the previous year, and in the village of Pinalejo. Matriculation included some of the older, more mature leaders of the churches. However, once again we faced the same dropout problem as the previous year. We discovered that the attractive murals and capsule lesson that I had presented in various congregations had given the impression that the mastery of the Bible was easier than it really was.

Nevertheless, we finished the year with roughly the same nucleus as the year before, plus a few more participants, although the center in El Progreso did show a slight decline. For the first time we had a missionary participant in the program, as Dr. Joyce Baker, M.D., having had no previous training, decided to enroll to receive some Bible training.

Several features of the Bethel Series seemed to appeal to the Hondurans: the emphasis upon learning to teach the Bible by actually teaching it, the rote memory of key biblical concepts, the bright murals. Those who applied themselves testified to having learned a great deal.

SPECIAL EVENTS

The year ended on a strong note with a convocation on the theme of Christian social action, with Jacinto Ordoñez, executive secretary of ALET, invited as the key speaker. A workshop for all students on all levels was held. Five of the correspondence students received certificates, including the wives of two pastors. Ordoñez, deeply impressed with the comprehensive program of theological education and the enthusiastic participation of the students, made only one suggestion.

He noted that although we were training a new group of pastors and many laymen, we had no program of continuing education for the present pastors. He warned of the possibility of a severe gap in the church emerging between older pastors and the present generation of students, both resident and extension.

This led to a program of continuing pastoral education for the following year. The Synod executive committee suggested that two short three-day courses be offered during the week when the pastors had to be in San Pedro for their monthly meeting. That, coupled with a wise use of the annual pastors' retreat and the sabbatical program, they felt, would do the needed job of continuing education.

SYNOD RELATIONSHIPS

Instead of beginning my annual report to the Board with a section on theological education, my usual practice, I began with a section on Synod politics.

During 1968, I had become acutely aware of the close relationship of theological education to Synod politics. I had written in my report: "The future of theological education is closely related to Synod politics. . . . This may be the key factor in our current adventure in theological education."[6]

Now, in 1969, I noted three areas where I felt we were in trouble with theological education, not so much internally, but rather in our relationship to the church which we professed to serve.

In the first place,

> . . . the residence program appears irrelevant because there is neither money to support new pastors nor are there vacancies for them to fill in the local churches. And under the present plan

6. Kenneth and Ann Mulholland, "Annual Report—1968," p. 2.

there is no possibility to serve part-time until a congregation can support them full-time.[7]

Second, as the Synod's steadfast refusal to permit a tent-making ministry persisted,

> . . . the extension program is weakened because one of its major purposes—that of preparing future pastors within their community who would serve as student pastors over a long period of time while finishing their studies and building up the local church—is undercut. The possibility of church extension is extremely limited because we are polarized between 100% professional pastors and 100% volunteers. Thus, the extension program is reduced to nothing more than a good high-level lay training program.[8]

Third, it began to appear that not only did the resident program appear irrelevant and the extension program weakened, but also that preservation rather than growth was the goal of the church in the face of diminishing subsidy from the United States without a corresponding rise in membership and giving on their part.

> . . . I was apparently quite wrong in believing that Synod was interested in an approach to theological education that would aim to serve the needs of a growing church; rather, the interest seems to lie in the direction of a prestigious professional ministry for a static church with the gradual abandonment of a full ministry of Word and sacrament in the rural areas.[9]

In the light of developments the following year, my pessimism appeared overdrawn. During 1970 the church experienced a rise of 40% in church membership and 25% in stewardship.

Nevertheless, in spite of these gains, when the rewritten internal discipline of the church was submitted during the 1970 session of Synod by a committee led by the old guard, it called for prohibiting any person who occupies the role of pastor from engaging in secular work. In one sense this was an advancement. The old discipline, though largely ignored, had also prohibited the wife of the pastor from engaging in secular work!

---

7. Kenneth and Ann Mulholland, "Annual Report—1969," p. 2.
8. *Ibid.*
9. *Ibid.*

The tragedy of the new discipline lay in the fact that it still allowed only for lay volunteers and full-time professional clergy, with no intermediate category allowed, thus eliminating the possibility of tent-making ministers. However, not all were in agreement with this draft of the discipline and so it was returned to a committee for revision to be presented and voted upon in November, 1971.[10]

EVALUATION

The statistics indicating that 22 students completed a total of 153 quarter hours by extension point in the direction of consolidation. The extension program now appeared as an increasingly accepted facet of theological education. The extension students began to see themselves more and more as part of the Theological Institute. My own experiences were constantly broadening and Kenneth Trauger's insights and zeal were proving helpful. But I still did not feel that the extension program was deeply indigenized. It was still a missionary project.

---

10. The Rev. J. Cristobal Bustillo had gone on record as favoring a tent-making ministry. During 1968, he had offered to assume a position as a teacher in a primary school with the local church responsible to provide only a parsonage and minimal allowance to support his pastoral work. His petition was turned down by the Executive Committee of Synod.

Chapter XII

A YEAR OF BREAKTHROUGH: 1970

Vacations provide a chance for reflection. In addition to a time of much-needed recreation for my family, vacation provided an opportunity to gain a new sense of personal perspective in the light of the pessimism which had swept over me in the latter part of 1969. Four factors blended to provide that perspective.

PAUSE FOR PERSPECTIVE

The first factor was the publication of Ralph Winter's monumental anthology, *Theological Education by Extension,* which collected together all the important articles, speeches, and pamphlets that combined to form the literature of the extension movement. Previously many of these resources were scattered and difficult to obtain. Many of our efforts in Honduras, as well as elsewhere in Latin America, had been on the basis of trial and error with occasional ideas filtering across my desk from various countries and conferences to provide corrections to the defects in our own system. I devoured the 648 pages of this volume, jokingly referred to as "The Bible" by extension enthusiasts.

The second factor was the experience of living for nearly two weeks at the Theological Community in Mexico City. Into this ecumenical venture have been poured hundreds of thousands of dollars by the then six cooperating denominations: Episcopalian, Lutheran, Methodist, Disciples, Congregationalists (United Church of Christ), and Baptist. Each of the four seminaries has its separate, but adjoining, campus with a common dining hall and interchange of professors. My reaction was one of horror. For the purpose of academic interchange and dialogue with the university community, of which almost none existed, the Theological Community had been located in the wealthiest district of Mexico City in buildings noted more for their splendor than for their functionality. The overwhelming majority of the faculty (9 of the 16 full-time professors) were North Americans. The national churches made almost no investments in the Theological Community; in fact, some opposed it because the graduates could not serve effectively in any area except large urban or suburban centers, whereas much of Mexico is rural. The critiques of traditional theological education made by zealous extension enthusiasts hit the Theological Community point-blank.[1] I was overwhelmingly convinced that the type of theological training imparted there only widened the gap between clergy and laity. The visit served to underscore my convictions about extension.

The third significant experience was learning to know the Rev. Arthur Von Gruenigen, then acting dean of the United Evangelical Center, one of the four component seminaries at the Theological Community. Von Gruenigen, an experienced missionary keenly aware of the needs of the local church, concurred with the difficulties involved in the Theological Community. We spent many hours together as he tried to formulate the shape that an effective program of theological education for Mexico would assume. He had no previous experience and very little knowledge of theological education by extension. Yet, with his candor and insight, he provided a means of feedback and reflection for the ideas that I expressed to him—ideas which had been developing for some time. At the close of our time together in Mexico, I felt considerably enriched by the perspective of Von Gruenigen. He felt determined to return to the rural districts of Mexico where he had previously ministered, to establish a system of decentralized theological training. Latest reports indicate that he has been exceedingly effective in establishing such a system.[2]

---

1. Cf. the article, "Extension Theological Training in Mexico," *Theological Education Newsletter* (June, 1970), p. 2. This article, appearing in a National Council of Churches publication, underscores the same problems which I had observed. The conclusions were arrived at independently.

2. David M. Stowe, "Report of Latin American Visit," pp. 2-3. Unpublished confidential report; Arthur and Dolores Von Gruenigen, "Circular Letter dated December, 1970."

The final crucial factor was a meeting with Ross Kinsler in Guatemala on my way from Mexico to Honduras. Kinsler indicated areas in which Winter's anthology, which contained numerous articles written by him, was dated. He stated that recent experience indicated that more structure was needed in regional centers even with highly motivated students. He stressed the importance of brief weekly quizzes at the weekly encounters both as a diagnostic device and to insure student mastery of the cognitive material. He also pointed out that monthly regional meetings were proving impractical and that the experience of the Evangelical Presbyterian Seminary of Guatemala indicated that quarterly meetings were better. He also was able to provide me with much needed recently published material in pastoral counseling and Christian education.

RESTRUCTURING THE WEEKLY MEETINGS

On the basis of what I had learned during vacation time, we began to restructure the class time during our weekly gatherings in Honduras. Classes generally assumed the following order: a brief quiz, review of the previous week's assignment with the introduction of supplementary material by the professor, discussion and application, presentation of the assignment for the following week. Normally, 15 minutes were provided at the beginning of the session to attend to such things as prayer, Bible reading, singing, announcements, questions, and financial arrangements. Most students paid their fees on a monthly basis: 25 cents to matriculate and 25 cents per month for the nine-month course. This was the basic schedule:

6:15 p.m.	Church History (San Pedro Sula only)
7:00 p.m.	Devotions and Business Transactions
7:15 p.m.	Christian Education
8:15 p.m.	Break
8:25 p.m.	New Testament Survey
9:25 p.m.	Dismissal

GATHERING INTEREST AND SUPPORT

In the four continuing centers, total enrollment was lower than the two previous years, but drop-outs were almost nonexistent. No more than two or three persons who began did not complete at least one quarter of work. In all, 26 students completed a total of 267 hours by extension in Christian Education, New Testament Survey, and Church History.

Still another positive factor was the growing interest of nationals who desired to teach in the extension program: one pastor volunteered to teach theology whenever it was offered; another to teach Christian education; and a third to teach preaching and worship. One of the pastors, the Rev. J. Cristobal Bustillo, joined the center as a student intent on upgrading the formal theological training he had received 15 years previously.

Four nationals actually did take part in the teaching during 1970: Mrs. Benigna Figueroa, a primary school teacher, taught a quarter of educational psychology; Mrs. Rafaela de Radillo, a high school guidance counselor, taught a quarter on educational methods, as did Mrs. Gregoria de Aguilar; and Miss Lillian O'Dorle, a senior student in the residence program, also taught educational psychology in two centers. The Rev. Miguel Martínez began a class in educational psychology at the La Lima center.

Esprit de corps ran high as all students gathered for a special workship on Church Growth in Honduras, later for another on Christian Education, and finally for a retreat just prior to graduation. A choir was formed and displays from the Christian education courses were prepared. A growing sense of unity was noted among residence and extension students as both began to feel part of a single institution. In the minds of the students, the Theological Institute began to be seen not so much as a place, but as a community of students and teachers serving the same Church under a common Lord.

LOW-LEVEL PROBLEMS

One of the setbacks during 1970 was the disintegration of the lower-level training program utilizing correspondence materials. After an excellent beginning in 1968, the residence phase of the program was postponed, and when it was finally held attendance was cut in two in the aftermath of the "Hundred-Hour War" between Honduras and El Salvador during 1969. Nevertheless, about a dozen students did attend the two-week institute and many more continued their studies by correspondence.

During 1969 and 1970, static was developing between Trauger and the Synod. Trauger felt that the Synod was not making good use of the training the people were receiving. This was causing discouragement on the part of students who had made great sacrifices in some cases in order to attend. I had noted this in my 1969 report to the United Church Board:

> A serious problem is the unwillingness of some of the pastors and of Synod to recognize the leaders that come out of this program and the inability to use these persons due to the present structure of the church.[3]

Trauger, in protest, refused to make accustomed quarterly visits to the students. Still another problem developed when the 1970 institute, scheduled for the Yoro area alone, did not materialize due to the lack of agreement as to whether the local congregation in the area or the Theological Institute should take the initiative. As a result nothing happened at this level in 1970 except for a trickle of correspondence lessons which continued to be turned in.

Further problems confronted the correspondence aspect of the comprehensive program of theological education. The materials in use were constantly being upgraded by the Latin American Biblical Seminary, which produced them. While at one time they were ideally suited to persons who were literate, but with little formal schooling, they are now geared to almost a full Bible institute level and assumed as minimal a primary-school education. This means that curriculum was in need of radical revision.

I sought to sum up these difficulties in my 1970 report to the United Church Board:

> The lower level extension program under the supervision of Ken Trauger stagnated in its rural division due to misunderstanding between Ken and Synod, although some of the students faithfully plugged along by almost pure correspondence. Ken felt with some justification that Synod leaders were not using the personnel

---

3. Kenneth and Ann Mulholland, "Annual Report—1969," p. 1.

being trained and that therefore it was better not to train them. Added to this the correspondence materials which we have been using and adapting to our needs have been so upgraded the last couple of years as to be beyond most of our students.[4]

EVALUATION

As 1970 closed, it became apparent that due to lack of candidates the residence program was heading for extinction. Feeling that our continued presence in Honduras would only serve to impede the development of national leadership and was not necessary in the light of the phasing out of the residence program, the Board decided that we were not to return to Honduras.

The Rev. J. Cristobal Bustillo, who was already serving as interim rector during our absence, was elevated to permanent full-time rector. The residence program was closed down and the Theological Institute became an extension seminary. The two or three prospective residence candidates were given scholarships to study abroad at high-level theological seminaries.

Fortunately, Synod was able to absorb the members of the graduating class of 1970 because of the increase in giving and also because there were only four. One resident student had switched to the Church of the Nazarene before graduation. One of the five graduates had received some training as a practical nurse and was employed by the Medical-Social Department of the Association of Evangelical Institutions of Honduras. That left Synod with only three pastoral candidates and one Christian education worker to absorb.

However, I felt satisfied with the progress we had made in the extension system, as I pointed out in my 1970 annual report to the Board:

> Two of the twenty or so "steadies" have now completed the equivalent of their first year of theological studies. Among the biggest gains were the participation of four Honduran teachers in the extension program, the appearance of volunteers interested in teaching future courses, and the growing sense of community on the part of the extension students. Through such activities as a workshop on Church Growth, another on Christian Education,

---

4. Kenneth and Ann Mulholland, "Annual Report—1970," p. 3.

the formation of an excellent choir and a joint retreat with the resident students, they really began to feel themselves a part of the Theological Institute on a par with the residence students.[5]

PROSPECTS AND PROBLEMS

In November, 1970, at the annual Synod meeting, Bustillo enunciated eleven objectives which he hoped to realize as rector.[6] He announced his intention to follow the current system, modifying it slowly as he gained experience, in order to conform it to his announced goals. Synod gave him a vote of confidence. Bustillo also received extensive orientation for his new role.

Prospects for progress in extension theological education were severely dampened, if not dashed, when Bustillo suddenly resigned both as rector and pastor. The entire program of theological education was suspended for the year. It was too late to appoint and orient another new rector. Behind his resignation lay the following conflict: Bustillo was slated to devote full time to theological education, but with no residence program, Synod leaders felt that he could easily pastor a local congregation as well. Bustillo, rightly convinced of the need to give full time to the development of a theological education program, felt that the division of his time would result in mediocrity in both responsibilities and, deeply hurt at the Synod's reversal, resigned to assume a job as professor of Bible at the Evangelical High School in San Pedro Sula. A year later, he also resigned from the high school and convinced Synod to assign him without salary as pastor to the congregation in the distant town of Yoro, where he also taught in the primary school, thus becoming the first "tent-making" pastor in the Synod's history—and up until now the only exception to the Synod's stand against such a pattern of ministry.

At the close of 1971, the Rev. Jorge Jacobs, a patriarch of the national church, was named rector. Aged and unable to travel extensively due to ill health, he was also burdened with heavy administrative and pastoral responsibilities. He indicated that under these

---

5. *Ibid.,* p. 1.
6. Bustillo's objectives are outlined in a paper whose translated title is, "My Words as Interim Rector of the Theological Institute," pp. 1-2.

circumstances an extension program was out of the question, but he would assume the responsibility for directing the resident studies of the young man and two young women who desired to study for the ministry. He carried out that responsibility faithfully until November of 1974, when at the graduation of the three he announced the Institute board's decision to close the Theological Institute and use the money saved to send qualified candidates with their secondary education complete to the Central American Theological Seminary in Guatemala City. Three candidates were chosen and sent for 1975.

At the annual Synod meeting, the decision of the Institute board was reversed by the delegates, who voted to suspend the work of the Theological Institute only for 1975, rather than discontinue it.

Future prospects for theological education by extension in the Evangelical and Reformed Church of Honduras became dependent upon at least three other factors in addition to naming another person or persons to coordinate or supervise the program of theological education.

First, without a residence program, it appears wise to affiliate the few extension centers with a recognized seminary such as the Evangelical Presbyterian Seminary of Guatemala. Another possibility is the formation of a national, interdenominational extension seminary for Honduras. At present the Mennonites, Conservative Baptists, World Gospel Mission, and Four Square Church have all begun flourishing extension programs.

Second, for maximum effectiveness, there is need to organize and supervise a definite plan of field work for extension students. This plan can best be supervised by local pastors, but not without orientation from the head of the extension program.

Third, the tightly knit centralized structure of Synod needs to be loosened, with more responsibility passing to the local congregations to encourage and recognize local leaders. A regular place needs to be made for volunteer and part-time clergy, as well as locally supported student pastors. At present Synod structure remains musclebound rather than flexible in ministering to the total spectrum of classes and masses in Honduras, although recent overtures do indicate a renewed interest in extension under national leadership.

Part IV

Concerns That Can't Be Avoided

Chapter XIII

CHURCH GROWTH: A MEASURING ROD
FOR THEOLOGICAL EDUCATION

Up to this point, this book has sought to analyze the factors which bear upon theological education in Latin America; to trace the historical development of the theological education by extension movement; and to relate personal experiences having to do with the development of such a program in Honduras. However, there remain a number of concerns related to theological education by extension which, although not central, keep coming up and do require discussion. Five such concerns are: church growth, pre-theological education, accreditation, the role of the teacher, and the relationship between residence and extension theological education.

What is the relationship of church growth to theological education by extension?

CHURCH GROWTH DEFINED

Church growth means three things: qualitative growth, organic growth, and quantitative growth.

Qualitative growth is the process of morally, intellectually, and spiritually perfecting those who have been added to the church. Dr. Ralph Winter writes: "*Qualitative* growth relates to or derives from the degree to which the will and ways of a church are conformed to the image of Christ."[1] Orlando Costas takes Winter's definition of qualitative growth a step further by distinguishing between conceptual and incarnational growth. The former refers to the extent of awareness

---

1. Ralph Winter, "Theological Education and Church Growth: Will the Extension Seminary Produce Church Growth?" *Church Growth Bulletin* V (January, 1969), p. 339.

which a community of faith possesses in regard to the understanding of its nature and mission in the world. It includes the knowledge of biblical facts and theological concepts. The latter refers to the degree of involvement of a church in the life and problems of the society in which it finds itself.[2]

Organic growth has to do with the degree of improvement that there may be in the organizational structure of a church as it seeks to fulfill its discipling and perfecting mission: the system of relationships among its members expressed in its form of government, financial structure, leadership style, kinds of activities in which its time and resources are invested. For instance, a church can be said to have grown organically when it has scattered its thousand members in groups of a hundred in ten strategically located centers, each with its own pastor; rather than have the 1,000 members collected together in a single congregation with two or three pastors.

The third component of church growth is quantitative, ". . . made up of a whole series of numerical components, each of which may vary independently for separate reasons. . . . The net numerical growth is the summing up of all these positive and negative components."[3] Positive components include ". . . gains by the baptism of the children of church members (biological growth), gains by conversion of non-Christians, the restoration of those who have fallen away, gains from members arriving from other churches."[4] Negative factors are ". . . losses due to deaths, losses due to reversions, losses due to transfer of members elsewhere."[5]

THEOLOGICAL EDUCATION: INSTRUMENT
FOR CHURCH GROWTH

Winter affirms the growth of the church as a major means by which the effectiveness of theological education can be measured.

---

2. Orlando E. Costas, *The Church and Its Mission: A Shattering Critique from the Third World* (Wheaton, Ill.: Tyndale House Publishers, 1974), pp. 87-149. It is important to note that while theological education by extension has been influenced by the church growth movement and does take seriously the importance of holistic church planting and development it is not a captive of any single concept of the church's mission.

3. Ralph Winter, *op. cit.,* p. 340.   4. *Ibid.*   5. *Ibid.*

The degree of quantitative growth plus that of organic or qualitative growth all together constitute the scale on which we should measure the results of theological education whether of the conventional type or the extension variety.[6]

From Costa Rica, the voice of Prof. Victor Monterroso adds:

. . . growth is an experiential phenomenon inherent in the life of the Christian Church. This suggests to us that theological education ought to be a means for such growth. . . . to speak of growth, we mean not only the numerical addition to the body of Christ, but also the deepening of the knowledge of God. . . .[7]

The pragmatic criteria espoused by Winter and Monterroso are relatively new in theological education, which has generally measured the effectiveness of its endeavors in terms of the academic quality of its graduates.

A. Clark Scanlon specifically proposed this viewpoint as long ago as 1962, even before the origin of theological education by extension. In a small book, *Church Growth Through Theological Education,* written out of his own background as rector of the Baptist Theological Institute in Guatemala City, he examines the growth rate and basic leadership training programs of the various denominations at work in Guatemala in the context of the geographical, historical, social, and cultural reality of that nation. After setting forth those principles of theological education which are conducive to growth, he discusses the problems involved in the implementation of such an approach. He concludes with some concrete and positive suggestions about where to begin and how to proceed.[8]

While Scanlon thinks primarily in terms of residence training and lay programs, he does deduce several principles which have been taken into account in the development of theological education by extension, such as the importance of responding to the leadership training needs of the homogeneous units that make up the church

---

6. *Ibid.*
7. Victor Monterroso, "El Crecimiento de la Iglesia y la Educacion Theologia (sic), *Monografías Teologia y Vida,* p. 1.
8. A. Clark Scanlon, *Church Growth Through Theological Education,* pp. 1-62.

without dislocating these persons from the "mosaic of peoples, classes, and languages in Latin America . . ." to which they belong.[9]

Monterroso, Read, and Johnson cite theological education by extension as a pattern of ministerial training worthy of study because of its significance for the growth of the church. However, Winter is quick to point out that the employment of extension methodology by itself will not automatically produce church growth, unless concern for the propagation of the faith and the multiplication of churches is built into the thinking of those who plan and execute theological education by extension.[10] He goes on to suggest four guidelines the extension seminary can follow to promote growth consciously.

Seek Leaders Significant for Church Growth

First, it will seek to train leaders who are already significant for church growth. With its flexibility the extension seminary can consistently seek out from among various subcultures those churchmen whose habits, convictions, determinations, and God-given gifts are actually promoting the extension of the Church. Winter defines these men as those who are already effective propagators of the gospel.

> . . . those significant for church growth are already winning men to Christ, already running branch churches, already conducting prayer meetings and Bible study in their own homes and other centers. . . . When some bright man applies who has *not* opened any branch Sunday school, *not* preached at any street corner, *not* gone out regularly to a likely ward of the city or village in the mountains to conduct worship with a couple of families of believers, *not* distributed tracts, and *not* invited outsiders to church meetings, let him be told to remedy this gap in his credentials and apply again next year.[11]

Winter not only advocates that admission to the extension seminary be based upon a person's work for the advancement of the Gospel, but that continuation in the program be based upon the same thing. He

---

9. William R. Read, Victor M. Monterroso, and Harmon A. Johnson, *Latin American Church Growth*, p. 333. Pages 326-338 deal specifically with ministerial training.
10. Winter, *op. cit.*, p. 340.
11. *Ibid.*, p. 341.

writes that monthly reports indicating "that what is learned is being passed on to unbelievers is an essential part of extension."[12]

Adapt Programs to the Subcultures Served

Second, it will adapt its program to each subculture it serves, as it writes its books and creates its curriculum. This task goes beyond the functioning of different academic levels. While theological education by extension by its very nature has an enormous reach which can embrace many subcultures, this will prove self-defeating if it tries to force all who study into the same mold, even though it attempts to do so without extracting them from their own environment. Therefore, the curriculum needs to include variations which focus the attention of the real leaders on ways to communicate the Gospel and multiply churches within each distinct subculture.

Build Church Growth Theory into the Learning Process

Third, it will build church growth theory into the very learning process of the program and into the students themselves. While students are often taught how to run existing congregations—especially those in low-middle-class urban areas—many seminaries offer no solid course to every student on the procedures, methods, special trials, dangers, and delights of starting a church from scratch. More than a decade ago Scanlon dealt with this matter for residence programs when he suggested that some courses be bypassed and the focus of others changed.[13] He also counseled the re-evaluation of present principles and procedures in terms of church growth: the shortening of courses; the simplification of operation and curriculum to make possible a larger percentage of the institutional support by national funds; the utilization of experts in church growth (both from within the nation and from abroad) through special courses; the deployment of students in field education assignments not only to assist a pastor in his shepherding task, but to help him begin new work; the creation of a climate of perennial evangelism and expansion; and the increase of lay training outreach through regional

---

12. *Ibid.*   13. Scanlon, *op. cit.*, pp. 49-50.

institutes, short evening courses, correspondence courses, and special units for monolingual Indians.[14] Winter calls for such a close integration between field experience and study that the study is actually a part of the work of fomenting church growth and a portion of student evaluation is based upon how successful he is in that labor. He suggests that in order to pass a course a student reteach its basic content to a group of laymen in his congregation. "What about a course which teaches a student how to start a brand new congregation and requires that he teach the course to five apprentices,"[15] he asks.

Employ Professors Who Are Church Planters

Finally it will seek professors who are themselves church planters. Winter and Scanlon agree that it is important to have faculty members intellectually convinced of the supreme importance of communicating the Gospel, and personally involved in the outreach of the church. Roger S. Greenway notes the favorable effect that professorial participation in door to door visitation has upon his students:

> . . . the benefits to the work and the effect that it has on the student's enthusiasm for visiting increase immediately when their "maestro" is doing it too.[16]

My experience confirms the boost in morale of the student body when professors work side by side with students in the diffusion of the Gospel, whether through tract distribution, Bible sales, or direct door to door evangelism. Scanlon urges that theological training schools make better use of pastors who display great practical skill in local church planting and development.

In summary, Winter challenges extension seminaries to incorporate church growth elements into their developing personnel, structures, programs, and teaching methodology.

> . . . the extension method can wed the worship of the true God and the traditional academic essentials to hard, bold plans for full-orbed Church growth! Conversely, the extension seminary,

14. *Ibid.,* pp. 56-62.
15. Winter, *op. cit.,* p. 342.
16. Roger S. Greenway, "A Church Planting Method That Works in Urban Areas," *Evangelical Missions Quarterly* VI (Spring 1970), p. 54.

if it simply teaches courses and gets men over academic hurdles can easily be a failure. It might even withdraw the real leaders of the churches from vital communication of the Gospel and set them to Bible study and at worst to climbing the mountain of educational respectability. This tragic outcome can be avoided. It will take resolute and speedy action during these days of the formation of the extension seminary to build church growth emphases into every aspect of the curriculum, and pedagogy, and practice of the extension seminary. Extension can be a vital means of dramatic forward movement *if it will accept the harness of the Great Commission.*[17]

CHURCH GROWTH THROUGH EXTENSION CHAINS

George Patterson has already been mentioned in this book for his creative way of adapting the principles of theological education by extension to the needs of rural persons with limited education. With the mind of an educator and the heart of an evangelist he skillfully blends education and evangelism. His work is an outstanding example of the way theological education by extension can be related to church growth. Theological education by extension for Patterson is more than a program to decentralize a traditional residence seminary; it is an instrument for planting new churches.

"Let's multiply churches through extension chains," urges Patterson in a 1974 article appearing in the *Extension Seminary.*[18] An extension chain, according to him, "is the process of church reproduction in which a mother church with an extension center starts one or more daughter churches which in turn become extension centers and start more churches."[19] He cites the example of the Baptist Church in Olanchito, Honduras, which raised up several daughter churches through its extension program. One of these raised up four more congregations. One of those four grand-daughter churches raised up still another church (great-grand-daughter) in a nearby village which in turn is raising up other churches nearby. "It took

---

17. Winter, *op. cit.,* p. 342.
18. George Patterson, "Let's Multiply Churches Through Extension Chains," *Extension Seminary,* no. 3 (1974), pp. 1-8.
19. *Ibid.,* p. 1.

from between three months to two years to add each link to the chain."[20]

Not an advocate of spiritual "lone-rangerism," Patterson gives strong emphasis to the place of the local congregation in church growth.

> The links are not individual witnesses, but congregations. The most effective unit for spiritual reproduction is the local church. An individual should witness for Christ as an arm of his own congregation. Making obedient disciples as demanded by the Great Commission requires a team effort. Persons with different spiritual gifts work together. The *body* reproduces itself. The daughter church inherits the seed of reproduction from the mother church to produce granddaughter churches.[21]

The principal of the extension chain, missionary or national, is the key. Both educator and church planter, the chain begins with him. He is the person who initiates and directs the flow of activities, ideas, and of the reteachable materials, self-teaching textbooks made especially for in-service training of a pastor, who in turn teaches the materials to his church or to his own extension students who may teach the same studies the following week to their own students in other subcenters.

> He may be the only teacher in the chain with previous theological education. His students become extension teachers under his direction as soon as they have begun raising up their first daughter church. For example, the [principal] of the chain in Honduras teaches three student-workers in two centers. These men teach the same materials to another 20 men in eight subcenters in daughter churches. Some of these 20 pastors-in-training teach another 25 men in more remote villages. The chain provides pastoral training in 30 congregations. To make the outer links grow and multiply requires edifying teaching all the way along the chain and thus helps the older churches to keep growing, too.[22]

Qualities suggested for a principal of an extension chain include pastoral experience, extension know-how including the ability to secure or write reteachable materials geared both to the student's progress and to his churches' needs, evangelistic vision, and the re-

---

20. *Ibid.*   21. *Ibid.*   22. *Ibid.*, p. 2.

sources and willingness to travel. The willingness to work under the local churches is essential, for the extension chains are anchored into the very life of the local congregation. It is also essential that the principal visit and observe regularly all the works in the chain, in order to counsel and prepare reteachable materials for their current needs. Planning is also an essential part of his responsibility. He must know his field of responsibility culturally, geographically, and socially. Then he must draw up a clear strategy to start new congregations of obedient disciples in every unevangelized locality within the defined area of responsibility. The overall plan then needs to be broken down realistically into easy, workable steps which fit into the time and budget of the principal.

Nothing takes the place of example. Therefore, the principal himself, working closely with a believer who has close friends or relatives in an unevangelized community, raises up the first daughter church himself. Patterson warns against the use of ". . . special campaign methods, public invitation, loud speakers, special tract campaigns or any other gimmick, until you and all your students have fully mastered the fundamentals of personal, effective witnessing."[23] The principal continues evangelizing until he has baptized several men. Then, after these men have started witnessing, Patterson suggests that an extension center be formed in the church and that one or two of the men be enrolled to be "trained *in* the work, not *for* it." The class should be small for detailed coverage of the students' needs.

> One or two is best. More than four will result in another Sunday school class. In each class you must deal with the details of each man's church work; you can't do this with a crowd.[24]

Patterson suggests that the men be local, mature family men—the kind of men Paul, in his Pastoral Epistles, recommends for leadership —and warns against matriculating single young men for an extension chain. As most missionaries can testify, single young men tend to produce a dead-end "preaching point" with mainly women and children in attendance. Patterson does not discount illiterates as leadership material, provided they have the respect of the community.

---

23. *Ibid.*, p. 3.   24. *Ibid.*

You may have to teach your student to read. Don't hesitate to train a humble uneducated peasant if he is typical of his group. . . . Such men make the best lay pastors for people of the same social group. They identify. They also make the best extension teachers for training other lay pastors of the same social class.[25]

Patterson emphasizes that the new student worker be mobilized to raise up his new congregation from the very beginning. "Break this rule and you break the extension chain," he warns. "You will have only a preaching point instead of a church; a sure dead-end link."[26] This means that a good part of the extension class is given over to a discussion of the practical work of the student. Teaching must be geared to his immediate needs. His needs take priority over the lesson plan that the teacher would like to present.

The churches which are founded, like the whole extension program in Olanchito, are obedience-oriented. Patterson summarizes the obedience that Christ requires of his church in seven general headings: repentance from sin, baptism, practical love, the Lord's Supper, prayer, giving, and witnessing. Trying to avoid the cultural overhang which plagues so much cross-cultural missionary endeavor, Patterson tries to stick to basics. He distinguishes sharply between the divine commands which are universally binding upon the church, apostolic practices, and evangelical traditions. While apostolic practices, such as traveling by boat, serving the Lord's Supper daily in homes, speaking in strange tongues, baptizing converts immediately upon profession of faith, cannot be prohibited, neither can they be commanded as binding upon the church. Evangelical traditions cannot be commanded either, for they have not been given by divine revelation, but have arisen out of historical situations. Thus, such things as the use of choir robes, Sunday school, resident seminaries, preaching outlines, raising the hand to accept Christ, the use of a pulpit, traditional denominational requirements for baptism and ordination must be discarded if they are culturally irrelevant or impede simple, immediate obedience to the commands of Christ for His churches. Patterson counsels:

---

25. *Ibid.*, p. 4.
26. *Ibid.*

> Direct all your teaching toward helping your student obey the simple commands of Christ for His churches. Never start a daughter church with detailed bylaws inherited from a mother church in a different area or you will produce a dead-end link. An extension chain will cross social and language barriers with little problem if you limit the new church requirements to the mere commandments of Christ.[27]

The training of the leaders for these new congregations is gradual. The teachers in the extension centers and subcenter begin by teaching their students to witness more effectively. From there they go on to teach their students how to prepare new believers for baptism, organize the church, learn discipline, and serve the Lord's Supper. Preaching is one of the last things students are taught, rather than one of the first, contrary to the practice in many programs of theological education, both residence and extension.

> New believers should not preach. They can sing, pray, read the Bible and give testimonies. Until there is someone ready to preach, the Lord's supper should serve as the center of their worship. It will not corrupt new believers to serve the Lord's supper, but it will swell their heads to preach. Let their preaching develop naturally out of their witnessing. First they will win their friends by humbly presenting Christ with their own Bibles. Soon they begin telling their friends Bible stories. Then they teach simple Bible studies using the reteachable extension materials. Gradually this practice in communicating the Word evolves into preaching avoiding the stilted preaching manner provoked by premature pulpit assignments.[28]

Patterson places before his workers the importance of following Christ's teaching patterns. He urges them to teach primarily by their own personal example, motivating their students through the use of an obedience-oriented curriculum which allows students to progress at their own speed and insures that each week's study produces the most urgently needed practical work.

Another task of the extension principle is to help each newborn daughter church become a mother church as well by urging it to mobilize its workers for continued reproduction. This will probably

---

27. *Ibid.,* p. 5.   28. *Ibid.,* p. 4.

involve the opening of a subcenter, which can then be placed under the direction of a capable extension student, who now advances to assume the role of student-teacher.

> Not every student has this capacity; but try them. The slower man may surprise you. It helps little to be bright if one cannot take heavy responsibility. Once he realizes that he stands at the head of a new section of the chain, a mediocre student will often start new churches with a zeal and facility which surpasses his teacher. But keep out of his way when he takes his first solo flight. Do not control his movements; let the work get out of your hands. Let him reteach the same studies which he has learned from you to his own new students (II Tim. 2:2). Let him repeat everything he has seen you do, in the same way. He does not need to complete the entire pastoral course before he opens his own subcenter; he needs only to keep a unit ahead of his students. He teaches them what is still exciting in his own experience.[29]

Such a program demands constant evaluation of the progress of each student and teacher in the extension chain. Checklists, detailed analyses of dead-end links, and regular visits to all centers are indispensable to effective work. At the same time, the principle must maintain a constant search for student teachers to repeat the process by which new links are formed in the extension chain.

The growth of extension chains in rural Honduras is but one example of how theological education by extension is a powerful instrument in the hands of the educator-evangelist who will place himself into the hands of God's Holy Spirit to bring about healthy, growing churches.

---

29. *Ibid.*, p. 6.

Chapter XIV

PRE-THEOLOGICAL EDUCATION

The matter of pre-theological education is almost inseparably tied to any responsible discussion of theological education.

The usual procedure of theological training institutions is to demand certain educational prerequisites for entrance and depend upon the public or private institutions of the nation to provide the required educational base. In the case of theological schools which require university training for entrance, there is often a recommendation, at times even a certain required course of study, which must be followed. In the case of theological schools which require secondary education or less, course requirements are not generally specified because most curriculums in Latin American countries at both the primary and secondary level, even in private schools, are largely determined by rigidly defined government standards. Electives are at a minimum.

Theological education by extension aims to educate the real leaders of the church without sacrificing the ideal that a pastor have some base of general education. This helps to equip him for a leadership role among the people to whom he ministers. Coupled with the ideal of some general education as a base for theological study, there is also the hard fact that persons without at least a primary education fail at extension study because they do not have sufficient reading ability to do the large quantity of outside reading, programmed or otherwise, demanded of students in an extension setting. There are, however, some notable exceptions which challenge this premise. The Anglican Extension Seminary in northern Argentina has developed an outstanding course on pastoral theology aimed at the fourth grade level. Entering students need only the ability to read and write. However, by the time he finishes the course the student should have developed the intellectual capacity to do secondary-level work—even without having earned a primary school diploma. Thus, though simple, the course is not superficial and has been used with good results among university students as well. It consists of five programmed compendiums based on the life of Christ as found in the Gospel of St. Matthew. To date the course has had remarkable initial results in terms of both student interest and church development. More than 7,000 copies of the initial volume have been sold. In Honduras, George Patterson has demonstrated that extension education can be effective with semi-literate peasant farmers. Out of his experience in Colombia, Wayne Weld has stressed the strategic importance of low-level training, and Bolivia's William Kornfield has come out strongly for an obedience-oriented approach to theological education by extension at the lower levels. Current interest in nonformal education also holds much promise for the future of such training.

My experience, however, confirms the necessity of primary education in order to satisfactorily complete extension studies. In several cases, perhaps as many as ten, the pleas of local pastors resulted in the admission of persons who had not completed their primary education into the extension program of the Evangelical and Reformed Church in Honduras. In all cases except one, they failed to keep up with the class and withdrew in failure. Winter states: "Seminary courses if they were to amount to anything require reading skills, for example, which these men simply do not have."[1]

Even in a day when the world of technology is upon the nations and is not going to hold back until they get ready for it, 83% of the adult population of Latin America has had less than a primary education.[2] Despite the contribution that evangelical churches are making and have made in the field of adult education, a study in Guatemala revealed that only 20% of all adult Protestants had completed primary

---

1. Ralph Winter, "Pre Theological Education," *Theological Education by Extension*, p. 56. These and other articles by Winter on Pre-Theological education first appeared in *The Evangelical Seminary* I (July, 1966), pp. 1-4.
2. Eulalia Cook, "Alfalit: Strategic Instrument for Latin American Believers," *Evangelical Mission Quarterly* VI (Spring, 1970), p. 161.

school.[3] And this is more than double the percentage within the general population. Does not extension education, by usually requiring the minimum of a primary education, automatically eliminate many of the leaders it claims it desires to equip?

While a seminary in a developed nation can set standards and leave the initiative totally to the student, because the society offers a wealth of opportunities for the achievement of those standards, most developing nations are so limited that theological institutions are often forced to choose between the following alternatives: lower their standards, eliminate almost all the prospective leaders, or help students get the prerequisites they lack—which in general means at least a primary education.[4]

Fortunately, many extension leaders, determined neither to lower the standards nor give up the vision of educating the real leaders, have opted for the third alternative: help students get the needed prerequisites.

What are some of the possibilities for pre-theological education up to full primary level (and beyond in some cases) for mature adults— many with families and jobs?

There are five basic paths, some more feasible than others: return to day school, special tutoring arrangements through day school, evening school, pre-theological education by extension, and Alfalit.

DAY SCHOOL

The most obvious path is to return to day school. It is not uncommon to see persons in their late teens seated in a primary school classroom because they started school late, have decided to return, are attending only alternative years to allow other family members to attend, or having received the third grade education—all that was available in their part of the country—are now returning to complete their education as the government adds three more grades to their school.

---

3. Ralph Winter, "Summary of the Questionnaires," *Theological Education, by Extension,* pp. 65-69.
4. Ralph Winter, "The Theme of This Issue," *Theological Education by Extension,* p. 65.

However, attendance at day school precludes the holding of a job and is often degrading to a mature adult. Furthermore, it is universally recognized that the pedagogical methodology useful in teaching children basic subjects is ill-adapted to adult psychology. Also, only one year at a time can be completed.

TUTORING

At times tutoring arrangements are possible. One mission school had a plan whereby adults officially enrolled in the day school, but never attended class. They did assignments at home and spent an hour or two a week with the teacher of their grade for purposes of clarification. Then at the end of the year, they took the government final examination for their grade. The manager of the Evangelical Bookstore in San Pedro Sula, Honduras, completed his final three grades of primary school in two years via this route. I know one young farmhand who completed the sixth grade while finishing his first extension course.

NIGHT SCHOOL

A third option is evening school. Increasingly, both private and public schools are offering the full six grades of primary school. Some are offering secondary education as well. Classes generally run from 6:00 to 10:00 P.M. in Honduras. Hours may vary some from nation to nation. Unfortunately, such schools usually exist only in major urban centers and larger towns.

The entire primary school curriculum is taught almost exactly as it is in the day schools. It takes an entire year to pass a single grade. Classes are largely a repetition of the government program for children. Little concession is made to adult psychology or adult capacity. Thus, adults in second grade, for instance, have to take second-grade sewing, second-grade music, and second-grade art as well as the major subjects, for which they use the same texts employed in the day schools. Only very recently have a few governments begun to make adjustments and allowances in the direction of adapting their curriculums and teaching systems to genuine adult education. Costa Rica, for instance, allows adults to earn their secondary diploma by passing a series of sufficiency examinations administered by the government. A number of private academies have sprung up to prepare students to pass the exams through a year of intensive evening study, regardless of how many years of secondary education one has previously completed.

Many adults are attracted to these evening schools simply because other adults are involved too. Thus, they do not feel out of place, despite the faults of the schools. Furthermore, the evening hours permit one to work during the day. However, the drop-out rate is extremely high, usually about 50%, and many schools count on it by demanding payment in advance, to make a good profit.

I was acquainted with a tailor and a book store clerk who were getting their pre-theological education in this manner, one on a primary level and the other at a secondary level.

EXTENSION

A fourth method to provide pre-theological education was initiated by Dr. Ralph Winter, while he was a missionary in Guatemala. It continued under the direction of Mr. Richard Cuthbert, a Presbyterian missionary educator. It now functions under the supervision of Colegio La Patria High School, located in Quetzaltenango.

Dr. Winter simply applied extension principles to pre-theological education, employing regional centers, weekly encounters between students and teachers and workbooks aimed at guiding personal study during the week. Its major innovation lies in the preparation of books for each major subject that take the student directly from first through sixth grade. It is a vertical rather than a horizontal structure.

The books are 8½ x 11, with printing on one side of the page only, ranging from 130 to 160 pages. Each book takes up one of the major subjects and follows it through the first six grades. We did not print one book for each grade, but printed a book on each subject, taking all six grades of that subject in the same book. The usual book for fourth grade, for example, repeats most of the third grade math. Our math book, for example, does not repeat anything, but takes up, say fractions and runs straight through, the more advanced paragraphs on fractions being clearly labeled as "fourth grade," "fifth grade," sixth grade, etc. The five books are Math, Language (i.e., Spanish), Natural Science, Social Studies, and Health. Another reason for this system is the fact that the adults are at all levels. Some may take two years while others in only six months can pass the tests necessary for their diplomas. Some need to cover everything, others only a part, and many need to go further back in one subject than another. For an adult the diploma is the target, and so all of them need books that go through the sixth grade. These books are not just workbooks, but present subject matter as well as questions.[5]

As can be seen, instead of necessarily studying all subjects for a given grade level, the student studies a single major subject from first through sixth grade. The government permitted the elimination of minor subjects. He then takes the government exam for that subject. When he has successfully passed the entire government primary exam he receives his certificate. As of 1972, more than 750 students were enrolled in the Guatemala program. In the first three years, more than 100 received their diplomas. Forty of them went on to enroll in seminary.

Backed by about a dozen missions, churches, and educational institutions, this extension system, although originally designed to provide pre-theological education, was called the Lincoln Cultural Union. This is because Lincoln, one of the most respected North American heroes to Latin Americans, studied at home as an adult. Entrance continues to be open to all—regardless of religion, age, or sex. The Union has recently been phased out. Responsibility for the administration of the program passed to the Presbyterian High School, Colegio La Patria, located in Guatemala.

Although successful in Guatemala, one difficulty with the exportation of the program lies in getting international recognition for the books used in Guatemala. Requirements for a primary certificate vary from nation to nation, and the hypersensitive nationalism current in many Latin American countries will not tolerate the references in the books to a Guatemalan setting. This means rewriting and reprinting not only the social studies book, but many other subjects

---

5. Ralph D. Winter, "The Problem of Pre-Theological Training," *Theological Education* by Extension, p. 55.

which make indirect reference to the Guatemalan scene, a highly expensive process. Because the "accrediting agency" is the government of each nation rather than a regional association, it is difficult to have a single text receive international recognition. Thus, when the Association of Evangelical Institutions of Honduras sought permission to use the program there, the government turned them down unless all books were rewritten to Honduran government specifications, which was prohibitive in terms of both cost and personnel.

ALFALIT

The final path for consideration is the newly developed adult primary education course developed by Alfalit, a Christian organization which teaches people to read and follows up with Christian literature and programs of community development. The name "Alfalit" is formed from two Spanish words: *alfabetizar,* to teach to read, and *literatura,* reading material.

Alfalit began by producing low-level literature only, until it was discovered that newly literate persons usually lapsed back into illiteracy when they did not have simple reading materials or could not yet read the newspaper easily.

Educators, working closely with Alfalit, pointed out the possibility of continuing education for newly literate adults right up to sixth grade. Alfalit responded to the challenge. Recently a curriculum was finished which completely covers average primary school requirements both horizontally and vertically so a person may study math, for instance, all the way from first to sixth grade before going on to science; or he may study all the subjects of a given grade at the same time.

In this sense the Alfalit materials are not dissimilar to those produced by the Lincoln Cultural Union. However, because of its international scope and reputation, Alfalit has been able to secure the cooperation of various Latin governments which have promised to recognize their course of study as having primary school equivalence.

Alfalit methodology is a cross between extension education, night school, and tutoring. While the texts are to a large degree self-teaching, the centers may meet as often as every night or as little as once a week. Whether groups will be paced or individuals allowed to progress at their own rate appears to vary from place to place.

Alfalit is very congenial to the evangelical cause in Latin America. If it is able to continue to receive the support of nearly all the governments, it may provide the needed continent-wide breakthrough in pre-theological education.

Such a breakthrough would go a long way toward furthering the cause of theological education by extension: helping the natural leaders who are prospective students to get needed prerequisites without lowering minimum standards, at the same time preparing these persons for the self-directed study needed for theological education by extension.

Chapter XV

ACCREDITATION: THE QUESTION OF EQUIVALENCE

One way to maintain the quality level of a training program is through the mutual stimulation and challenge of some kind of formal or informal regional association of institutions which are involved in the same kind of training. The awareness of the standards and efforts of the rest of the group helps each school to strive to realize the objectives and aspirations that it has chosen for itself. Also, the sharing of problems and solutions is of great benefit.[1]

Despite growing tendencies during recent decades toward cooperation within the evangelical movement in Latin America, this unity was late to show itself in the sphere of theological education.

HISTORICAL SURVEY

Although there were some personal conversation and communication among various seminary rectors, the first firm step was taken in 1961, when teams from the newly founded Theological Education Fund made a survey of theological education in Latin America through local or regional conferences held in 21 different countries.[2] The results of the study were published under the title *The Christian Ministry in Latin America and the Caribbean,* edited by Dr. Wilfred Scopes. Among the recommendations was one calling for the formation of national and regional theological associations.

Brazil moved quickly and in 1961 the Association of Evangelical Theological Seminaries (ASTE) was formed. Meanwhile, in San José, Costa Rica, the Latin American Biblical Seminary wanted to

---

1. Ralph D. Winter, "An Extension Seminary Manual," *Theological Education by Extension,* p. 413.
2. Wilton M. Nelson, "Una Breve Historia de la Associación Latinoamericana de Escuelas Teologicas (Region del Norte)," p. 1.

award the Th.B. degree, but the directors of the Latin America Mission refused permission unless the seminary either was recognized by the American Association of Theological Schools (AATS) or a similar association was formed in Latin America to confer recognition upon the degrees which the seminary would grant. Dr. Wilton Nelson, then rector, wrote to Dr. José Miguez Bonino, rector of the Evangelical Faculty of Theology of Buenos Aires, asking him to write a circular letter to all Latin American seminaries citing the necessity for the formation of such a theological association. In 1962, he did send out such a letter to the leading seminaries.

During 1963, two consultations were called and financed by the Theological Education Fund. Out of these grew the South American Association of Theological Institutions (ASIT) and the Latin American Association of Theological Schools—Northern Regions (ALET). The latter was born on March 22, 1964, as the Latin American Association of Biblical and Theological Institutions (ALIBT), a multi-level association. The Evangelical Theological Association of Bolivia (ABET) was later formed as a national association and finally expanded to include Peru and Ecuador, as the Andean Association of Theological Education (AADET). A national Mexican Association of Evangelical Theological Institutions (AMIET) has also been formed within ALET.[3] The latter two groups have failed to function effectively.

THE PRESENT SITUATION

The introduction on a wide scale of theological education by extension has brought about the necessity to rethink the basis for accreditation.

For two of the regional associations, ASIT, which includes the southern cone of South America, and ASTE, which takes in Brazil, this poses no major problem. Both tend to confine their interest to upper-level, high-quality, residence academic institutions. They use much the same standards as those used in the United States.[4] ASTE

---

3. Cf. 1971–72 Directory of ALET.
4. Ralph D. Winter, "An Extension Seminary Manual," *Theological Education by Extension*, p. 413.

incorporates exclusively those schools which require a high level of academic prerequisites for admission, while ASIT allows for members on two academic levels. However, only the upper-level members can vote.

On the other hand, ALET, which incorporates Gran Colombia, Mexico, Central America, the Caribbean, and recently Spanish-speaking schools in the United States, "has encompassed from the very start three different academic levels with voting right for all in the plenary sessions, with voting on accreditation matters being carried out by the schools of each particular level.[5]

ISSUES RAISED BY EXTENSION

There are four major issues confronting the extension seminary movement at present which are being discussed and debated in the accrediting associations—particularly in ALET and AADET. They have to do with terminology, functional equivalence between levels, academic equivalence between residence and extension seminaries as well as between diverse extension seminaries, and finally theological tensions.

Terminology

The problem in terminology centers around the use of the word "seminary." There is a growing tendency in Latin America, particularly among members of ALET and AADET, to use the word "seminary" to refer to any ministerial training institution regardless of the academic level at which it functions.[6]

Previously in Latin America, the term "seminary" had been reserved for university level theological training institutions which admitted only those students who had completed their full secondary studies. A "theological institute" was a ministerial training school at the secondary or university preparatory level, which required the completion of three years of secondary or middle education for admission. A "Bible institute" was a ministerial training institution which had a prerequisite of primary education for entrance. A "Bible school" was

---

5. *Ibid*.
6. Ralph D. Winter, "What's in a Name?" *Theological Education by Extension*, p. 62.

a primary school level institution which built its studies only upon the assumption that its students were literate.

Frequently, however, in my experience, what happened was that institutions called themselves what they hoped to be rather than what they really were. Thus, the Evangelical Presbyterian Seminary of Guatemala (while still a purely residence program) hoped to limit students to those with their full secondary education completed; but they had to lower their standards to ninth grade and even sixth grade on some occasions in order to muster enough students to continue to operate. The Theological Institute of the Evangelical and Reformed Church of Honduras hoped to admit no one without at least a ninth grade education, but never succeeded in having all but a small minority of students who had completed more than sixth grade. The neighboring Honduras Bible Institute of the Assemblies of God began with third grade although they eventually hoped to make a sixth grade education the minimum—some day.

Scanlon tried to broaden and at the same time sharpen these definitions when he, following in a modified manner Keith Hamilton's classification system, defined the levels as followed:

> The term theological education is used to include Bible Institutes, Theological Institutes, and Seminaries. . . .
>
> *Bible School:* This school usually has a four to nine month school year in permanent buildings. It generally has some resident staff. While the graduates probably will be paid workers, some may be unpaid. The school has low prerequisites in education.
>
> *Theological Training School:* This institution is a Bible School with high prerequisites in education (at least grade school, often two or three years of high school). It usually has a nine month session.
>
> *Theological Seminary:* This grade of training takes in college graduates or men with a year or two of college.[7]

Those who favor the use of the term "seminary" for all institutions where ministers of any church are trained, appeal to etymology, history, and predicated practical results.

---

7. Scanlon, *op. cit.,* pp. v-vi. Cf. Wilfred Scopes, ed., *The Christian Ministry in Latin America and the Caribbean,* pp. 222-226.

Etymologically,

> . . . the word "seminary" means "seedbed" and . . . doesn't really indicate any academic level: it means a place where you train ministers. . . .[8]

Historically,

> The name gained currency in the Roman Catholic tradition after the Council of Trent, and was finally adopted by U.S. Protestants in the past century. Its original meaning was "seedplot" and referred to the special formation of certain persons for the special role of the priest or ordained minister . . . any school is a seminary that offers the special training needed by the ordained pastor of a congregation. It has nothing to do with levels of education.[9]

And practically,

> Every place ministers are trained is going to be called seminary. . . . Mind you there are many classes of seminary degrees. We plan on giving six different kinds eventually. . . . This will reduce the false hierarchialization of ministers many of us have been accustomed to and that we would like to try to abolish.[10]

As of this writing the debate over terminology continues with no resolution in sight.

Functional Equivalence

Faced with the desire of the extension movement to define the word "seminary" in purely functional rather than academic terms, ALET from its beginning set up a system of accreditation aimed at including institutions on all levels. The first assembly in 1965 recognized three levels of titles.[11]

Licenciatura was the title awarded to a student who had successfully completed four years of university level theological study after meeting the entrance requirement to the university in his country.

---

8. Peter Wagner, "Panel: Existing Programs of Seminary Extension Training," *Theological Education by Extension,* p. 352.

9. Ralph D. Winter, "An Extension Seminary Manual," *Theological Education by Extension,* p. 381.

10. Wagner, *op. cit.,* p. 353.

11. "Acuerdos Hechos Sobre Acreditación." A mimeographed document setting forth the accreditation standards of ALET.

Bachillerato was to be awarded to those who had completed at least three years of theological study at the university preparatory level after having successfully completed the middle or secondary education requirement of his respective nation.

Diploma was awarded upon the completion of three years of secondary level theological study after having successfully completed primary school.

In addition to the educational level of the student body, accreditation of degrees was based upon the number of full-time professors, library facilities, plus other requirements added in subsequent annual assemblies of ALET.

For various reasons the accrediting program of ALET based on these standards was never fully implemented. Did accreditation imply acceptance of degrees of other institutions only or did it include individual courses leading to those degrees? What about low full-time professor to student ratio (1:41 in the Evangelical Presbyterian Seminary of Guatemala; 1:30 in the Theological Institute of Honduras) due to the large number of part-time extension students? What about institutions which did not even require primary education for entrance —could a Certificate of Theology be accredited?

There is at present some effort to redefine the levels even more closely than the three previously mentioned, thus building three years of theological education (or its equivalent by extension) upon the following educational base for the following degrees: Doctorado—university licenciatura; Licenciatura—two years of university; Bachillerato A—full secondary including unversity preparatory; Bachillerato B—ninth grade; Diploma A—sixth grade (full primary); Diploma B (or Certificate)—third grade, possibly bare literacy.

Speaking of what this would mean, Peter Savage remarked:

> It doesn't matter if a student has had secular studies on a third grade secular level; he gets a seminary degree. Now mind you there are many classes of seminary degrees. We plan on giving six different kinds eventually. But they are all degrees from the George Allen Theological Seminary.[12]

---

12. Wagner, *op. cit.,* p. 352.

In review, ALET and AADET opted for functional equivalence. They held that at least three different levels of study should be accredited as valid for the training of a man who would be recognized as a minister by God's church upon the completion of any one of the three levels, should he meet the other requirements of the ordaining body.

Academic Equivalence

A third issue in the relation of the extension to the accrediting associations is the matter of the equivalence of structured academic units between residence and extension programs in the light of the once-a-week classes common to the extension pattern. Although Winter speaks of the many variables determining what goes on in the classroom, he continually stresses one constant: the system of basing "hours of credit" on hours of study. Although a credit hour originally referred to a class hour, today in advanced education it "likely refers not to the number of class hours, but the number of structured hours of student study, in and out of class."[13]

After an elaborate explanation of how these structured hours of student study are calculated, Winter concludes,

> Thus in a seminary program a credit or a unit or an hour ought to have the same meaning in study hours whether the work is done by extension or in residence. If a traditional ministerial course in a U.S. seminary required three years with 30 semester units per year, this is translatable into 3 years x 30 units x 45 study hours— 4,050 hours of work. Unless an extension program wants to run the risk of losing all standing for the credit it gives, it must, I believe maintain that kind of equivalence.[14]

He goes on to explain specifically how this relates to an extension program.

> The three year curriculum consists of thirty semester long courses. A semester course has a 1½ hour class each week and includes 1½ hours of outside study per week for five days of the week.

---

13. Ralph D. Winter, "An Extension Seminary Manual," *Theological Education by Extension*, p. 415.
14. *Ibid.*, p. 416.

This makes 9 hours a week for 16 weeks which is 135 hours, and when multiplied by 30 courses gives the sacred number, 4,050 hours, which we calculated above for the U.S. seminary. If anyone asks why we do this arithmetic, our answer is the same as Jesus' response to those who asked Him if He needed to be baptized: It is necessary to fulfill all righteousness."[15]

Winter's emphasis on class hours was, and in some cases still may be, important in helping extension educators to overcome inferiority complexes and reassure residence sticklers. However, in the last year or so, the matter of hourly equivalence has become less an issue due to the worldwide academic revolution which is beginning to recognize the value of non-formal education, even to the point of giving up to a year of university credit for knowledge and skills acquired in daily life. Accrediting efforts are now moving toward an assessment of the results of education rather than its processes. The question of equivalence then becomes not a matter of how many hours you have studied, but of what you now know and what you can now do.

In short, the accrediting effort is now moving toward an assessment of the results of education rather than its processes, in an attempt to translate educational reality into social commitment.

Theological Tensions

A fourth problem is that of the existence of theological tension among the various training institutions. While some important groups of conservatives have had in mind the organization of a distinctively conservative accrediting association which would have a doctrinal statement that would exclude the liberal institutions, the majority feel that the existence of theological accrediting associations including the entire spectrum is a more normal and healthy situation.[16] However, in order to avoid doctrinal problems this would necessarily limit the activities of the accrediting associations strictly to the academic aspect of the work rather than include the theological as well.

Such activities as a joint theological journal, exchange of pro-

---

15. *Ibid.*
16. C. Peter Wagner, "Debate on Accreditation and Associations," *The Extension Seminary and the Programmed Textbook,* p. 24.

fessors, theological conferences, etc., would most likely alienate important groups of conservatives, who while they might be willing to associate with liberally-oriented institutions for strictly academic ends, would not do so if the association carried what for them would be interpreted as theological implications.[17]

This problem is most acute in ALET, where diversity among member schools is greatest. AABET, which apparently is not functioning at present, was predominantly conservative in tone, while ASIT and ASTE, by excluding all but high-level institutions, which some interpret as a smokescreen for theological bias against conservatives, tend to be more liberal.

One extremely interesting development is the formation of an association in Brazil exclusively for extension seminaries, AETTE. Although this association is actually complementary to ASTE, for ASTE does not concern itself with either extension education or lower level training, theological overtones may become increasingly apparent due to the conservative coloring of AETTE and the liberal orientation of ASTE.

In 1973, the Association of Latin American Institutions of Theological Education by Extension was organized along lines similar to AETTE. Although a leftward drift in ALET is definitely discernible, the theological factor was not the principal reason for the formation of the new association. Rather, ALISTE leaders felt a need to concentrate exclusively on extension on a continental basis in Spanish Latin America, an impossibility within the regional limits imposed by the structure of ALET.

In summary, although sharp divergences of theological opinion do exist among Latin American Protestants, it does appear that liberal and conservative churchmen can cooperate in regional accrediting associations, provided that theological issues are subordinated to academic concerns and that ASTE and ASIT show more interest in recognizing the functional equivalence of ministerial training done both on a multi-level basis and by extension.

---

17. *Ibid.*

Chapter XVI

CATALYST: THE ROLE OF THE TEACHER

Because theological education by extension calls for a different style of education, it also demands a different kind of teacher. The effective extension teacher must be a catalyst rather than a depository of information which he dispenses to passive listeners in carefully prepared lectures.

INTERACTION WITH THE MATERIAL

Recalling the split-rail fence analogy for theological education by extension, cognitive input is received not during the fencepost seminars, but rather between class meetings and parallel to field experience. The interaction with the material to be learned takes place by guided personal study through the workbooks or programmed textbooks during the week. Part of the catalytic task of the extension professor is to ensure that this interaction does take place. This can be accomplished in several ways.

First, it can be encouraged through weekly or bi-weekly quizzes which, though brief, cover both objective and subjective (content and thought) aspects of the lessons for the week and relevant material previously covered. This practice tends to add a dimension of seriousness to the study, keep the student on his toes, and serve as a diagnostic device.

Second, interaction can be stimulated by a review of the students' workbooks. Students are required to answer all questions in writing. Some professors collect all assignments at the close of the class period and personally analyze the work of each student. This takes a great amount of time, although it is almost universally appreciated by the student. Often the student is required to write those notes which he has taken during the class period with a different colored marker from the one he has used to complete his assignment, so that the professor can see how much was completed before class and how much was done in class. Still other professors rapidly review the workbooks immediately after the weekly quiz, checking for completion of the assignment and marking in red anything that has been left blank. Periodically, they may collect and peruse the workbooks in order to get a general idea of student progress, but depend more on discussion and the quizzes as well as the final examinations for evaluation.

Third, the professor can ensure that such interaction takes place by personally confronting the students. The fairly informal seminar atmosphere with the resulting interaction enables the professor to take students aside and privately confront them should lack of preparation be a real problem. This is one obvious advantage that extension has over correspondence.

Fourth, the professor can encourage interaction with the materials through both review and preview. A common problem in extension education is that beginning students with limited academic background often cannot discriminate between those facts and concepts of primary value and those of secondary value. Dr. Harold Alexander gives great priority to this task.

> The first thing that the teacher has to do, in my opinion, is to tie things together. I think you are all aware of the fact that average students tend to get lost in the mass of detail. He doesn't often see the whole picture; he doesn't tie things together. This is something that the teacher in this system must do for the student. One of his roles is to make sure that the student continually sees the whole picture. The teacher reviews and previews in each class period. He tells the student where he has been. He goes through what is being done, and tells you where he is going. At the same time the teacher acts as a resource person.[1]

Then, as class time runs out, the extension professor passes on to a preview—sometimes highlighting the contours of the material to be covered the following session or throwing out key questions to be kept in mind while working through the material at home. In some

---

1. Harold Alexander, "The Use of Teachers in an Extension Program," *Theological Education by Extension*, p. 331.

courses, such as Christian Education Methods, it is a good idea to give the students a few minutes at the end of the class period to actually begin their assignments for the coming week to see if any difficulties are initially encountered, as well as to stimulate interest through foretaste.

Here, in limited doses, the use of lecture methods can be helpful—to survey and amplify material covered in the home study material.

INTERACTION WITH PEOPLE

As catalyst, the extension professor must not only help the student to interact with the material, but also with his fellow students and with his life situation. Mental agility and skill in discussion—in drawing out of other people the resources which they bring to the situation —is essential for effective teaching.

Following the quiz, checking of assignments, and review, the professor characteristically asks the students for questions they would like to discuss that may have risen out of the assignment material. Questions may be of a factual or interpretive nature. If none are immediately forthcoming, he may then ask students to answer specific questions which he senses are germinal. As discussion develops the field experience of the students generally comes into play and a genuine interplay of the material studies and life situations develops. Alexander describes this process:

> And we teach our class on a group dynamics or seminar approach. We start with the basic questions that are in the guide, but we never stop there. They are merely a springboard to get into the discussion. If you ask the question that is in the guide of the student, you get a start for an answer and then with other questions you make him develop it. You make him see where you can go with it, what you can do with it, and get a good discussion going with the students. We want them to see the implications in their subject, to be able to evaluate it, to be able to discuss it, to be able to bring their experience to bear upon what we are doing.[2]

During the discussion, the catalytic role of the professor may

---

2. *Ibid.*, pp. 330-331.

express itself either by helping the students to help one another or as a resource person himself. Because of the multi-level nature of extension training and because veteran students and beginning students are generally combined in the same class, the professor can help the entire class to experience mutual edification by enabling the advanced students and those with wider experience to counsel, advise, interpret, and share with newer students. Not only are students often very receptive to what they receive from their peers, but students learn to edify the persons in their congregations by actually edifying those in their class—by bringing their resources and insights to bear on specific matters through which they have already passed. Through this broad experience, the professor is also able to bring his own insights to bear upon the problems under discussion and to recommend other resources—books, persons, or audio-visuals upon which the class may draw.

INTERACTION WITH THE INSTITUTION

As catalyst, the professor is the visible representative of the institution. So he is an administrative link between student and institution and a means of interaction between them. The professor involved in theological education by extension generally has certain administrative responsibilities. Not only does he have to keep records of both grades and attendance, but finances as well. Registration, the sale of materials, keeping student and travel accounts are part of his routine. He is required to write monthly reports, course evaluations, and an annual report. He is also responsible to make announcements and either coordinate or lead brief pre-class worship or Bible study. Decentralized theological education requires sound administration if it is to avoid disintegration or dissolution.

INTERACTION WITH DIFFERENT DISCIPLINES

As catalyst, the extension seminary professor needs to be a generalist to interact with disciplines other than his own. "There is no way you can be an effective teacher in this system and be a narrow specialist," writes Alexander.[3] This, however, does not preclude being

---

3. *Ibid.,* p. 335.

a specialist in a given field; in fact, this is to be encouraged, but specialization should not be so constricted as to limit the professor's knowledge to a single field. From a practical point of view, the lack of available finances and personnel among the churches of the developing world almost insure that a professor will have to teach an occasional course out of his field. This need not be a traumatic experience. It can lead to a deeper and fuller integration between various fields to the enrichment of student and professor alike. Such an experience can aid the student to recognize that his professor, like himself, is a continuing student. Rapport is increased when the professor can say, "I don't know, but I'll do my best to find out by next week."

Although the above situation may be viewed as an impossibility if not absurdity in a traditional residence seminary, where each professor is viewed as an authority who must create his own course, it is not so in an extension, where the role of the professor is more that of a catalyst who helps the student interact with and apply material which he, the professor, may not have created, but which has probably been created by an expert in that field. After all, for students to have a New Testament man teach them homiletics may provide rich insights on the role of exegesis in sermon preparation; to have a theology man teach Christian education may open new dimensions in the communication of the faith; or to have a practical theology professor teach Old Testament may increase student awareness of the relevance of biblical materials to the complexities of church administration.

In summary, the role of the extension professor is to be a catalyst who interacts with his students so as to aid them in realizing their potential as thinking leaders who will accept new ideas and change, can put their theology into experience, will respect authority but not take its conclusions for granted, will question and think independently, and will not think they have arrived and are above their people.[4]

---

4. Gennet M. Emery, "Some Questions About Classroom Teaching" *Extension Seminary,* I (no date, but number), p. 3.

Chapter XVII

RESIDENCE AND EXTENSION: THE RELATIONSHIP

One of the perennial questions being raised in Latin American theological circles and ecclesiastical gatherings is that of the relationship between residence and extension, between centralized and decentralized theological education. There are four basic alternatives which may be characterized as follows: residence only, residence above extension, extension only, residence with extension.

RESIDENCE ONLY

The most simple, but also the most uncreative solution, is to ignore the entire extension movement and continue as in the past. However, even the most ardent defenders of the traditional system grant that the extension movement may serve as a corrective for some of the more obvious abuses that have crept into traditional theological education. Even such an ardent opponent of theological education by extension as Dr. José Arreguin, former dean of the Baptist Theological Education by Extension Seminary of Mexico concedes that extension:

> . . . reminds us that the task of proclaiming the good news and of evangelization belongs not only to the ministry, but to each member of the body of Christ. To prepare them for this work on its various levels is the task of the church through the teaching function of the Seminary. Also, it reminds us that the Church has her true work in the world and not inside of herself, as up to now we have been doing. . . .[1]

1. Dr. José Arreguin, "Reacciones a la Ponencia del Prof. Jaime Emery," 1. Translation by this writer. This paper, originally distributed in mimeographed form, has also been translated by Dr. Winter and appears in *Theological Education by Extension*, pp. 233-239.

RESIDENCE ABOVE EXTENSION

The second option is to maintain a strong residence program while utilizing the extension principle for lay training. Prof. Jacinto Ordoñez, executive secretary of ALET, expresses this point of view well when he writes: "An extension seminary offers us a method that I conceive of as applicable and functional for the preparation of the layman."[2] Such a program of lay training may be carried on in two ways.

Employing the extension pillars of guided daily study, weekly meetings at regional centers, and periodic gatherings of the entire student body, the centers may be taught by the pastor of the local church or by missionary or national specialists in theological education. In Costa Rica both the Methodist Seminary and the Biblical Seminary originally opted for extension education as a means of lay training. Both programs seriously floundered. The Rev. Rollin Dexter, former rector of the Methodist Seminary, informed me in a private conversation that the use of local pastors to lead centers in their own congregations failed because persons understood the program as just a more advanced midweek Bible study course, for which there was too much homework. However, a second attempt which enrolls the laymen as full-fledged students in the revived School for the Preparation of Methodist Workers numbered 141 students enrolled for 1975 and showed promise of future growth.

Although the Biblical Seminary skirted that problem by using missionary specialists as teachers, they discovered that many of the real leaders in the churches were not willing to make the sacrifices in time and effort for what they saw not as ministerial training, but as just another lay training program. They seemed to prefer the short-term Bible institute approach of two weeks or a solid month of study during a season of little other activity in rural areas. In the urban areas, the better-educated leaders were simply not challenged by another lay training program.

Thus, it would appear that unless extension education is presented as full-fledged ministerial training with transferable credits leading to

---

2. *Ibid.*, p. 2.

a diploma or degree from a recognized institution, it will not be taken seriously by the lay leadership of the church. Even Ordoñez later made a concession to his original statement, previously quoted, when he stated that he felt that perhaps theological education by extension could be a proving ground—a screening process—for candidates for residence study.[3]

EXTENSION ONLY

A third pattern is to dedicate oneself completely to extension and to close down the residence program. This is precisely what the Presbyterians in Guatemala did. They felt that their residence program was not economically justified by the results and that the efforts of the faculty and even the resources of the campus could be better utilized by exclusive dedication to training the leaders of their church in their natural setting. They have slightly modified that position by allowing occasional full-time students to reside on campus, although they too must study in the regional centers. One year some third-year extension classes were grouped during the middle of the week to allow students who have completed the first two-thirds of the program by extension, usually student pastors, to live on the campus Tuesday through Thursday to study by extension methodology, though in a residence setting. This enabled them to complete their studies more rapidly. Also, after having moved the campus from Guatemala City to the rural area and having sent extension professors on a weekly four-hour drive to the capital to man extension centers, they have now permanently moved one professor back to the capital, where he directs several regional centers.

Still other seminaries, more by necessity than by choice, have opted for a pure extension seminary. Lack of available funds for a residence program was the principal reason for founding the Center of Theological Studies in Quito, Ecuador, as an extension program. Lack of students was a main reason for phasing out the residence program of the Theological Institute of the Evangelical and Reformed Church of Honduras. Theological flack from a United States-

---

3. *Ibid.*, p. 3.

based mission board caused a denomination in one Latin American nation to close its heavily subsidized residence program in favor of a self-supporting national extension seminary.

RESIDENCE WITH EXTENSION

A fourth pattern is to maintain the traditional residence program, but supplement it with an equivalent extension program to reach those who desire a theological education but cannot attend the residence program. Rowen feels very strongly about the importance of a two-pronged thrust.

> The central school has several basic functions. One of the most important is to give the seminary's coherence and stability to the extension schools. The extension schools are not evening Bible schools or second-rate seminary programs. The students attending the extension centers are full fledged seminary students and they receive the same type of recognition upon completing their course of study as do the resident students. The only reason the extension centers can gain this standard of recognition is because it is part of an established school with a central location and campus. The extension centers bear the same name as the central school and every attempt is made to give each center the feeling of equality with the central school and to each other.[4]

This has been the pattern of such schools as the George Allen Theological Seminary in Bolivia, the United Biblical Seminary of Colombia, and the Evangelical Theological Seminary in the Dominican Republic, among others. It was the pattern of the Theological Institute of the Evangelical and Reformed Church in Honduras, as long as circumstances permitted. In my opinion, it is the most sensible of the four approaches.

Despite the weaknesses of traditional theological education, it does have certain advantages over theological education by extension. It provides the time and opportunity for concentrated and intensive study; ready access to professors; more-closely supervised practical work; motivation and facilities for depth study; a large library, audiovisual resources, office equipment; and a breadth of experience through

---

4. Samuel F. Rowen, *The Resident Extension Seminary: A Seminary Program for the Dominican Republic,* p. 16.

contact with students who come from varied backgrounds. Many would question seriously whether it is possible to train an elite of Christian scholars by extension. Further, some educators believe that urban youth eager to enter into a full-time church vocation are best trained in a residence institution.[5]

Rowen believes that the presence of an extension system may even improve the quality of the residence program within a given seminary.

> . . . the central school is now in a good position to avoid the great problem of having the classroom program geared to a student body with too great a range of educational background. . . . The (residence) school should concentrate on one level and would be most beneficial if it provided classes for those with high school and university training. It is these students who are most prepared for independent work and would benefit greatly from the advantages of full-time study with the use of the library facilities. Also, there are extra courses (e.g., Greek) which will be available to students on this level and are best studied under the close tutelage of a professor.[6]

Nor does he ignore the practical aspects of administration.

> The central school also provides a place for conducting the business that is associated with the school. In this type of program there is a great deal of material that must be prepared and duplicated. The need for faculty studies, conferences with students from the interior, board meetings, etc., are all provided for by the central school.[7]

Critics assail residence programs for not taking advantage of their full potential because of the immature character of an untested student body. But the presence of an extension system alongside a residence program can often alleviate this gap and reduce some of the apparent weaknesses of the traditional system. The superior inductive methodology and seminar type class sessions, whose value have been demonstrated in extension teaching, can be applied to residence programs as well. Furthermore, the residence students' contact with the often rough-hewn leaders of the local church, whose Christian experience and leadership ability are apparent, helps to

---

5. *Ibid.*   6. *Ibid.*, pp. 16-17.   7. *Ibid.*, p. 17.

bridge the generation gap and build fraternal relationships between present and future leaders. Finally, the periodic convocations serve to add enthusiasm and a dimension of fellowship not known when such special lecture series or workshops involve only the residence students and a few pastors.

Initial experience during the brief history of theological education by extension appears to show that there is a need to continue with traditional institutions. Where interchange between the two styles of theological education is encouraged, they can be mutually helpful allies in the monumental task of training leaders for the Church, not only in Latin America, but around the world.

CONCLUSION

Theological education by extension developed in response to the need to train indigenous Christian leadership in the context of the theological, ecclesiastical, geographical, anthropological, economic, and educational realities of Latin America.

From its unpretentious beginnings in Guatemala slightly more than a decade ago it has grown to include more than 10,000 students in Latin America alone. It is being adopted in nations as diverse as Portugal, India, Kenya, and the United States. Michigan State University Professor Ted Ward terms it "the largest nongovernmental voluntary educational development in the world."[1]

What some skeptics once termed a "fad" may, in fact, be precisely what Milton Baker, Conservative Baptist Foreign Mission Society secretary for Latin America and Africa, termed, ". . . the most significant development in theological education in the twentieth century."[2]

I believe that theological education by extension is not only a growing phenomenon, but a valid, viable, and valuable form of theological education. This thesis is supported by the following factors:

1. Theological education by extension takes into account the varied forms of ministry inherent in such historic patterns of training as apprenticeship, in-service training, and tent-making ministry, instead of trying to force all candidates into the mold of full-time, urban-oriented, professional scholar-pastor.

2. It allows a single school to work on more than one academic level and in more than one cultural sphere. It reaches out to the real

---

1. Cited by Ralph Winter, "The Acorn That Exploded," *World Vision* XIV (October, 1970), p. 15.
2. Cited by Samuel F. Rowen, "A Return to the Peripatetic School: The Extension Seminary," *Theological Education by Extension*, p. 139.

pastoral leadership of the church with first-rate theological education, allowing these men with high potential to become more than second-rate leaders.

3. It simplifies the structure and lowers the cost of theological education by adapting not only to the socio-economic conditions, but also to the cultural and educational patterns of the developing nations.

4. It incorporates modern educational principles, such as the "split rail fence" model, contextualization, and programmed learning into its educational theory. Learning takes place in the context of daily life. Thus, it gives promise to being able to train students to depend upon their own God-given resources for continuous, lifetime study.

These and other factors have converged to enable theological education by extension to overcome many of the disadvantages that have traditionally plagued residence programs in the developing nations, and to combine many of the strengths of other approaches to theological education without sharing their weaknesses. In this sense, theological education by extension is an idea whose time has come.

After studying 18 schools in Latin America which began extension programs, Dr. Baker observed, ". . . in every case those schools have a much higher enrollment . . . and the (quality of) students is significantly improved."[3]

Any system of theological education able to improve both the quantity and quality of theological education in any part of the world surely has a contribution to make in the development of the church and the fulfillment of Christ's Great Commission.

---

3. Cited by Ralph Winter, "A Revolution Goes into Orbit," *World Vision* XIV (November, 1970), p. 15.

BIBLIOGRAPHY

BOOKS

Allen, Yorke, Jr. *A Seminary Survey.* New York: Harper & Brothers Publishers, 1960.

Barclay, William. *The Daily Study Bible: The Acts of the Apostles.* Philadelphia: The Westminster Press, 1957.

Clark, Dennis E. *The Third World and Mission.* Waco, Texas: Word Books, Publisher, 1971.

Compendio de Teología Pastoral: Basada en la vida de Jesucristo en el evangelio según San Mateo. S.M. de Tucuman, Argentina: Seminario de Extensión Anglicana, n.d. 6 volumes.

Cook, Harold R. *Missionary Life and Work.* Chicago: Moody Press, 1959.

Covell, Ralph R., and C. Peter Wagner. *An Extension Seminary Primer.* South Pasadena, Calif.: William Carey Library, 1971.

Dillenberger, John, and Claude Welch. *Protestant Christianity Interpreted through Its Development.* New York: Charles Scribner's Sons, 1954.

Douglas, J. D., ed. *Let the Earth Hear His Voice.* Minneapolis: World Wide Publication, 1975.

Hill, D. Leslie, *Designing a Theological Education by Extension Program: A Philippine Case Study.* South Pasadena, Calif.: William Carey Library, 1974.

Hodges, Melvin L. *On the Mission Field: The Indigenous Church.* Chicago Moody Press, 1953.

Illich, Ivan. *Deschooling Society.* New York: Harper & Row, Publishers, 1971.

Jencks, Christopher, and David Riesman. *The Academic Revolution.* New York: Doubleday & Company, Inc., 1968.

Kelly, Robert L. *Theological Education in America.* New York: Charles H. Doran Company, 1924.

LaLive d'Epinay, Charles. *Haven of the Masses: A Study of the Pentecostal Movement in Chile.* London: Lutterworth Press, 1969.

Liggett, Thomas J. *Where Tomorrow Struggles to Be Born: The Americas in Transition.* New York: Friendship Press, 1970.

Niebuhr, H. Richard, in collaboration with Daniel Day Williams and James M. Gustafson. *The Purpose of the Church and Its Ministry.* New York: Harper & Brothers Publishers, 1956.

Paton, David M., ed. *The Ministry of the Spirit: Selected Writings of Roland Allen.* Grand Rapids: William B. Eerdmans Publishing Company, 1960.

Pomerville, Paul A. *Handbook for Theological Education by Extension.* North Sumatra, Indonesia: Assembly of God Publications, 1973.

Read, William R., Victor M. Monterroso, and Harmon A. Johnson. *Latin American Church Growth.* Grand Rapids: William B. Eerdmans Publishing Company, 1969.

Scanlon, A. Clark. *Church Growth through Theological Education.* Eugene, Ore.: Institute of Church Growth, 1962.

Scopes, Wildred, ed. *The Christian Ministry in Latin America and the Caribbean.* New York: Commission of World Mission and Evangelism, World Council of Churches, 1962.

Theological Education Fund Staff. *Learning in Context: The Search for Innovative Patterns in Theological Education.* Bromley, Kent, England: The Theological Education Fund, 1973.

————. *Ministry in Context: The Third Mandate Programme of the Theological Education Fund.* Bromley, Kent, England: The Theological Education Fund, 1972.

Wagner, Pedro. *¡Cuidado! Ahí Vienen los Pentecostales.* Benjamin Mercado, Trad., Miami, Fla.: Editorial Vida.

Ward, Ted and Margaret. *Programmed Instruction for Theological Education by Extension.* East Lansing, Mich.: Committee to Assist Missionary Education Overseas, 1970.

Weld, Wayne C. *The World Directory of Theological Education by Extension*. South Pasadena, Calif.: William Carey Library, 1973.

Winter, Ralph D., ed. *Theological Education by Extension*. South Pasadena, Calif.: William Carey Library, 1969.

Zorn, Herbert M. *Viability in Context: The Theological Seminary in the Third World—Seedbed or Sheltered Garden?* Bromley, Kent, England: The Theological Education Fund, 1973.

PAMPHLETS

El plan básico del programa de educación en América Latina y Las Antillas. Miami: Editorial Vida, n.d.

Ordóñez, Jacinto, ed. *Directorio de las Instituciones Biblicos-Teologicas de la Región del Norte de La América Latina, 1971–1972*. San José, Costa Rica: Publicaciones ALET, 1970.

Reynhout, Hubert, Jr. *The Bible School on the Mission Field*. Barrington: Barrington College, 1959.

Rowen, Samuel F., *The Resident-Extension Seminary: A Seminary Program for the Dominican Republic*. Miami: West Indies Mission, 1967.

Schlundt, Meta S., ed. *We Are Fifteen in Honduras*. St. Louis: Board of Foreign Missions, Evangelical and Reformed Church, n.d.

Twente, Theophil. *Honduran Rainbows*. St. Louis Board of International Missions, Evangelical and Reformed Church, Inc., n.d.

Winter, Ralph D., ed. *Extension Seminary and the Programmed Textbook—The Report of a Workshop*. Pasadena, Calif.: Publicaciones ALET, 1967.

PERIODICALS
(English)

"The ALISTE Project for Training Extension Specialists," *Extension Seminary*, no. 1 (1974), pp. 1-9.

Brainerd, Edwin. "The Myth of Programmed Texts," *Evangelical Missions Quarterly* 5 (July, 1974), pp. 219-223.

Cochran, David R. "Theological Education by Extension: What Can

It Offer the Churches in North America?" *Theological Education* 10, no. 4 (Summer, 1974), pp. 259-269.

Cook, Eulalia. "Alfalit: Strategic Instrument for Latin American Believers," *Evangelical Missions Quarterly* 6 (Spring, 1970), pp. 158-165.

Emery, Gennet M. "Some Questions about Classroom Teaching," *Extension Seminary* 1 (n.d.), pp. 3-6.

Emery, James. "The Preparation of Leaders in a Ladino-Indian Church," *Practical Anthropology* 10 (March–April, 1963), pp. 127-134.

―――. "Where Men Struggle to Study the Scriptures," *Presbyterian Life* 19 (October 15, 1966), pp. 14-15.

Extension: The Monthly Air Mail Newsletter, North Park Theological Seminary, Chicago (November, 1972 to present).

Extension Seminary, Seminario Evangelico Presbiteriano, Apartado 3, Rev. San Felipe, Guatemala, C.A. (1966 to present).

Goff, James. "Exalt the Humble," *Risk* 7, no. 2 (1971), pp. 30-36.

Greenway, Robert S. "A Church Planting Method That Works in Urban Areas," *Evangelical Missions Quarterly* 6 (Spring, 1970), pp. 152-157.

Hopewell, James F. "Guest Editorial," *International Review of Missions* 56 (1967), pp. 141-144.

―――. "Missions and Seminary Structure," *International Review of Missions* 56 (1967), pp. 158-163.

―――. "Training a Tent-making Ministry," *International Review of Missions* 55 (1966), pp. 333-339.

Huegel, John E. "Combining Extension with Residence," *Extension Seminary,* no. 4 (1973), pp. 1-5.

Kinsler, F. Ross. "Definitions: What Is Extension," *Extension Seminary* 1 (n.d.), pp. 1-4.

―――. "Open Theological Education," *Theological Education* 10, no. 4 (Summer, 1974), pp. 234-245.

LaLive d'Epinay, Christian, "The Training of Pastors and Theological Education: The Case of Chile," *International Review of Missions* 56 (1967), pp. 185-192.

————. "The Training of Pastors and Theological Education," *International Review of Missions* 56.

Nida, Eugene A., and William A. Wonderly, "Selection, Preparation, and Function of Leaders in Indian Fields," *Practical Anthropology* 10 (January, February, 1963), pp. 6-16.

Patterson, George. "Modifications of the Extension Method for Areas of Limited Education Opportunity," *Extension Seminary* 4 (1972), pp. 1-5.

————. "Let's Multiply Churches through Extension Education Chains," *Extension* II, no. 7 (July, 1974), pp. 3-11.

Savage, Peter. "A Bold Move for More Realistic Theological Training," *Evangelical Missions Quarterly* 5 (Winter, 1969), pp. 65-72.

Schonberger, Ernest. "The Episcopalians' Weekend Seminary," *Church Growth Bulletin* 3 (July, 1967), p. 234. Condensed from the Los Angeles *Times,* March 11, 1967.

Sell, Kenneth. "Preparation of New Pastors," *Honduran Highlights* (September, 1963), p. 3.

Taylor, John V. "Preparing the Ordained for Mission," *International Review of Missions* 56 (1967), pp. 145-157.

Theological Education Newsletter (June, 1970), pp. 1-4.

Thorkelsen, W. B. "Paintings Teach the Bible in Depth," *Eternity Magazine* 17 (March, 1966), pp. 26-28.

Wagner, C. Peter. "A Promising Breakthrough in Latin America," *Church Growth Bulletin* 4 (November, 1967), pp. 261-263.

————. "Seminaries Ought to Be Asking Who as Well as How," *Theological Education* 10, no. 4 (Summer, 1974), pp. 266-274.

Ward, Ted. "The Split Rail Fence: An Analogy for the Education of Professionals," *Extension Seminary* 1, no. 2 (n.d.), pp. 4-7.

————. "Theological Education by Extension: Much More Than a Fad," *Theological Education* 10, no. 4 (Summer, 1974), pp. 246-258.

Ward, Ted, and Samuel F. Rowen. "The Significance of the Extension Seminary," *Evangelical Missions Quarterly* 9 (Fall, 1972), pp. 17-27.

Weld, Wayne C. "The Current Status of Theological Education by Extension," *Theological Education* 10, no. 4 (Summer, 1974), pp. 225-233.

————. "Extension Education Seen as Meeting Needs of Churches," *Evangelical Missions Quarterly* 10, (January, 1974), pp. 48-53.

Winter, Ralph D. "A Revolution Goes into Orbit," *World Vision Magazine* 14 (November, 1970), pp. 14-16.

————. "Agonizing Reappraisal at the Quiche Bible Institute," *Church Growth Bulletin* 4 (March, 1968), pp. 287-289.

————. "Cultural Overhang and the Training of Pastors," *Church Growth Bulletin* 4 (November, 1967), pp. 260-261.

————. "Designing the Right Kind of Ministerial Training," *Church Growth Bulletin* 3 (July, 1967), pp. 230-231.

————. "New Winds Blowing," *Church Growth Bulletin* 3 (July, 1967), pp. 241-242.

————. "The Acorn That Exploded," *World Vision Magazine* 14 (October, 1970), pp. 15-18.

————. "The Extension Model in Theological Education," *Extension Seminary,* no. 2 (1973), pp. 1-6.

————. "Will the 'Extension Seminary' Promote Church Growth?" *Church Growth Bulletin* 5 (January, 1969), pp. 339-342.

PERIODICALS
(Spanish)

Berquist, James A. "Ministerio Rural y E.T.E. en la India ¿Un Caso de Potencialidad no Realizada?" *Seminario de Extensión,* no. 2, pp. 1-4.

Emery, Jaime H. "Bases de Extensión Número 1: Estudio Propio," *Seminario de Extensión,* no. 2 (1971).

————. "Educación por extensión y programación," *Seminario de Extensión,* no. 4 (1971), pp. 1-3.

————. "Centros para Estudios sobre la Educación Teologica y el

Ministerio: Una Propuesta Preliminar," *Seminario de Extensión,* no. 1 (1975), pp. 1-7.

Kinsler, F. Ross. "Definiciones: Lo que extensión no es," *Seminario de Extensión,* no. 3 (n.d.), pp. 1-6.

―――. "Extensión: Un Modelo alternativo para la Educación Teologica," *Seminario de Extensión,* no. 3 (1973).

―――. "La Metodología de la Educación Teologica por Extensión," *Seminario de Extensión,* no. 1 (1971), pp. 1-6.

―――. "Una Primera Evaluación del Proyecto de ALISTE," *Seminario de Extensión,* no. 2 (1974), pp. 5-8.

―――. "El Proyecto de Intertextos en Español," *Seminario de Extensión,* no. 3 (1972), pp. 1-9.

Lores, Rubén, "Nuevo Día para la Educación Teologica en América Latina," *Seminario de Extensión,* no. 3 (1971), pp. 1-5.

Monterroso, Victor. "El Crecimiento de la Iglesia y La Educación Teología (sic)," *Monografias Teologia y Vida* (1968), pp. 1-4.

Sturz, Richard. "El Crecimiento de la Educación Teologíca por Extensión en Brazil," *Seminario de Extensión,* no. 4 (1971), pp. 4-6.

UNPUBLISHED MATERIAL
(English)

Deardorff, Darryl. "Administrative Structures for the Theological Studies Center" (mimeographed).

Emery, James. "The Presbyterian Seminary in Guatemala: Three Years Later 1966" (dittoed).

―――. "Report of Visit to Africa to Observe and Discuss the Problems and Progress of Theological Education by Extension" (typescript), May 20, 1975.

―――. Personal letter to James Goff (typescript), December 29, 1971.

Hernandez, Ulises B. "Development of Faculty, Including the Use and Need of Scholarships to Study in Other Institutions" (mimeographed).

―――. "To What Degree Has the Center of Theological Studies

Begun to Understand the Total Reality of Our Country, and Apply the Gospel to This Situation" (mimeographed).

Kinsler, F. Ross. "Guatemala's Extension Plan: A Revolution in Theological Education" (typescript).

————. Personal letter to James Goff (typescript), March 13, 1972.

Kornfield, William J. Personal letter dated March 20, 1975 (typescript).

Kreps, George. "Financing the Center of Theological Studies" (mimeographed).

McKinney, Lois. "TEE Services in Brazil: Purposes, Projects, and Products" (mimeographed, July, 1975).

Mulholland, Kenneth. "Multi-level Theological Education" (mimeographed circular letter).

Mulholland, Kenneth and Ann, "Annual Report: 1967" (typescript).

————. "Annual Report: 1968" (typescript).

————. "Annual Report: 1969" (typescript).

————. "Annual Report: 1970" (typescript).

Schaal, Herbert. "September, 1970, Revision of Fact Sheet on Our Argentine Mission" (mimeographed circular letter).

Soto, Onell A. "The Theological Ecumenical Library" (mimeographed fact sheet).

Stowe, David M. "Report of Latin American Visit, March 1-16 1971" (mimeographed).

Troutman, Stuart I. "Theological Education by Extension" (typescript).

Von Gruenigen, Arthur and Dolores. "Christmas Letter" (Xeroxed circular letter), December, 1970.

Weld, Wayne. Personal letter dated February 27, 1975 (typescript).

Wagner, C. Peter. "Theological Education by Extension (mimeographed).

UNPUBLISHED MATERIAL
(Spanish)

ALET Boletín, publicado por la secretaria ejecutiva de la Asociación Latinoamericana.

Arreguin, José, Jacinto Ordóñez, Louis Weil, and Carlos Vore, "Reacciones a la Ponencia del Prof. Jaime Emery" (mimeographed typescript).

Bustillo, J. Cristobal. Personal letter dated February 15, 1971 (photostat).

————. "Mis Palabras como Rector Interino del Instituto Teológico" (mimeographed report).

————. Personal letter dated March 4, 1971 (photostat).
Castellon Gallardo, Samuel, and Kenneth Mulholland. "Un Llamamiento al Servicio de la Iglesia en La Comunidad" (mimeographed).

Carvajal, Gonzalo. "La Preparación Teológica Tradicional, Comparada con La Preparación de Extensión, Los Materiales y Metodos Apropiados y La Necesidad de la Aculturación de la Enseñanza" (mimeographed).

Crouse, Merle. "Manera de Colaborar en la Preparación de Liderato para Las Iglesias Ecuatorianas" (mimeographed).

————. "Un Informe de lo Hecho hasta Ahora en el Centro de Estudios Teológicos, con Recomendaciones para el Futuro" (mimeographed).

Emery, Jaime. "El Seminario de Extension o Tradicional: Conflicto o Cooperación—Amigos o Enemigos" (mimeographed).

de Escuelas Teologicas, Región del Norte, 1968 to the present. Apartado 2053, San José, Costa Rica (mimeographed).

Hankins, Wesley G., compilador. "Introducción al Método Inductivo de Estudio Biblicos" (mimeographed).

Horning, Estella de. "Hacia un Pastorado Adecuado para Las Iglesias en el Ecuador" (mimeographed).

Hwang, C. H. "Reconsideración de la Enseñanza Teológica del

Ministerio en Las Iglesias Jovenes en el Día de Hoy" (mimeographed).

Minnich, Dale. "Applicación de materials del Desarrollo de la Comunidad para Programas del Preparación Cristiana" (mimeographed).

Mulholland, Kenneth. "Informe del Instituto Teológico . . . Noviembre de 1967" (dittoed).

————. "Informe del Instituto Teológico . . . Noviembre de 1968" (dittoed).

————. "Informe del Instituto Teológico . . . Noviembre de 1969" (mimeographed).

————. "Informe del Instituto Teológico . . . Diciembre de 1970" (mimeographed).

————. "ETE: estructura democratica; metodología integra; énfasis misional," Nov. 5, 1973 (typescript).

Nelson, Wilton M. "Una Breve Historia de La Asociación Latinoamericana de Escuelas Teológicas (Región del Norte)" (typescript).

Ordóñez, Jacinto. "Acuerdos sobre Cuotas" (mimeographed).

————. "Informe final de la Consulta sobre 'El Futuro de la Enseñanza Teológica en la América Central' " (mimeographed).

Padilla, Washington. "El Liderato que la Iglesia Evangélica en El Ecuador Necesita Ahora y en el Futuro" (mimeographed).

Quijada, Alejo. "Panorama de la Educación Teológica de la Iglesia Evangélica Peruana con enfoque en la Enseñanza por Extensión" (mimeographed M.A. thesis). Seminario Bíblico Latinoamericano, San Jose, Costa Rica, 1974.

Rivas, Mario. "Pautas para la Educación Teologica por Extensión para La Unión Bautista Boliviana" (mimeographed M.A. thesis). Seminario Bíblico Latinoamericano. San Jose, Costa Rica, 1975.

Sarabia, Rafael. "Preparación de Liderato Indigena" (mimeographed.)

Smith, W. Douglas, Jr. "Evaluación del Progreso hacia el cumplimiento de las metas del Departamento de Educación Teológica de la U.C.E." Report to the 19th national assembly of the Evangelical Christian Union held in Carachipumpu, Bolivia, November 1-3, 1974 (mimeographed).

Trauger, J. Kenneth. "Letter to Directors of Evangelical and Reformed Synod" in Honduras containing annual report dated November 23, 1966 (typescript).

Will, Juan. "Informe del Instituto Teológico Preparado para la XIV Asamblea General del Sinodo de la Iglesia Evangélica y Reformada de Honduras Marzo de 1965" (typescript).

————. "Informe sobre las labores del Instituto Teológico" dated March 7, 1966 (mimeographed).

Winter, Paul. "El Entrenamiento de Lideres" (mimeographed).

Zorrilla, C. Hugo, compilador. "Alternativas en la Educación Teológica: Exploraciones sobre educación no tradicional," San José, Costa Rica: Seminario Bíblico Latinamericano (mimeographed).